P9-DIW-413

GOD MOMENTS

WRITTEN & COMPILED BY
MICHELE ELENA BONDI

JOSEPH KARL PUBLISHING

NOT FOR RESALE

copyright © 2010 Michele Elena Bondi

First edition

Cover photo (unaltered) courtesy of Roseann Nieman.

Michele's portrait © Kathy Rizzo.

Cover design by Roseann Nieman, Niemanart Graphics, www.niemanartgraphics.com

Book design and layout by Erin Howarth, www.wildernessbooks.org

To order additional copies, please contact:

Joseph Karl Publishing

P.O. Box 80371

Rochester, MI 48308

or visit

www.Godisatworkinyou.com

The Scripture quotations contained herein are from the New Revised Standard Version Bible, copyright, 1989, by the Division of Christian Education of the National Council of the Churches of Christ in the U.S.A.Used by permission. All rights reserved.

Bottesi, Michele Bondi.
    God moments / written & compiled by Michele Bondi Bottesi. -- 1st ed.
    p. cm.
    Includes bibliographical references.
    ISBN-13: 9781935356097
    ISBN-10: 1935356097

    1. Theophanies. 2. Faith. 3. Spiritual formation.
I. Title.
BT128.B68 2010   231.7'4
                QBI10-600138

This book is dedicated to Nancy Carabio Belanger, Belinda Bondi, Rejeanne Buckley, Chris Camilli, Sharon Rose Cecil, Lynn Czar, Jim, Teresa Koempel, Gene Kortsha, Lucy, George Madrid Sr., Linda J. Perakis, Ted, and everyone who has shared stories of love, discernment, faith, healing, suffering, miracles, and forgiveness for the love of God and one another.

God is at work in you!

CONTENTS

FOREWORD

God Moments—have you ever had one?
See them through the eyes of faith.

One day I took my children skateboarding at the local skate park. While paying the admission fee I was told that there was a woman upstairs in the viewing area who has six children. "Interesting introduction" I thought while proceeding upstairs to watch my children as they navigated the ramps. A woman was seated in the observation area. She was holding a baby and was surrounded by several young children.

We started talking and discovered that we have something in common besides absolutely loving motherhood—both of us are authors. We bought each others' books and I found her book of adoption stories to be so beautiful, faith filled, meaningful, and inspiring that I wrote a review. Meeting Coreen was certainly a God moment. Later I realized that our meeting was even more significant than I had first thought.

Little did I know when I met Coreen that God had started a sequence of events that would lead up to my next book. Originally my plan was to begin writing a book on the Eucharist after finishing two Catholic books for youth. As the days and months passed many people shared their inspiring accounts of extraordinary events with me. Then one day while talking to a friend outside the church after daily Mass, in the rain, I experienced another God moment. Right then and there I was given the assignment to write this book. At that time I also understood very clearly that certain events that occurred within the past year happened to prepare me for this book. That moment was so beautiful, because the great love that God has for every person was very obvious. He had me write and compile *God Moments* for you.

Even the front cover came to fruition through a series of God moments. I wanted the cover of the book to be very meaningful and reflect the significance of the stories that are shared in the book. I already had several images in mind to depict an appropriate metaphor for the grand and eternal picture that is created through our God moments. Soon after receiving the assignment I contacted my dear friend and gifted graphic designer Roseann Nieman. Roseann is the creative genius behind the images of Joseph Karl Publishing and Apostolate Films. Partnering with Roseann to create exceptional Catholic books was the result of another God moment. I was in need of a graphic designer and one day following Sunday Mass, Roseann approached me to say hello. During the conversation she mentioned that she was returning to work in graphic design. We have been working together ever since.

Right from the start Roseann told me she had the picture for the cover of the book. She also came up with the title. Although I was fond of my ideas, God gently encouraged me to let Roseann design the cover on her own. So I e-mailed her and gave her total artistic privilege. The day I met with Roseann to see her prototype cover of the book I was astounded, absolutely delighted, but not surprised. All along she knew that she had the picture for the cover of the book, which she took during a God moment while in a boat on a lake in Michigan. What do you see in the picture?

God moments are very significant experiences that have great meaning for us and for other people. They may involve people, animals, angels, saints, circumstances, or anything in God's creation. Always they involve an encounter with the Divine. Perhaps they are meant to challenge or change us, encourage and inspire us, motivate, comfort, or prepare us. Sometimes they occur over time for reasons that we do not immediately understand.

We can be confident that God always loves us, remains with us, and is our strength and our hope. Our mission is to know God and serve Him, always loving in greater measure. May the stories in *God Moments* help you to recognize these special moments in your own life and encourage you to consider their purpose.

—MICHELE ELENA BONDI
Holy Week, 2010

…for God,
all things are possible.
—Matthew 19:26

INTRODUCTION

Sharing the Love of God During
Very Private Public Moments

Love is deeply personal, sometimes very public,
always meaningful, and always necessary.

I will never forget the moment more than 20 years ago when I stood at the front of my church before so many cherished family members and friends and made one of the most important promises of my life. "I will love you and honor you all the days of my life." On the one hand I was overjoyed to be celebrating that joyful occasion in the presence of those who were so dear. On the other hand, the moment was very deeply personal and private yet was anything but concealed. That is how love is, deeply personal and also often very public, but always meaningful and always necessary.

I experienced a similar moment when my first child was born. There were so many strangers in the room to share our deeply personal, private, public moment as a new family. Some moments are private, like our time alone with God. Other times we experience very personal, private moments publicly, for example during the celebration of the Eucharist. We share these moments with people we know and also with people we do not know.

Last year my family and dear friends shared another deeply meaningful occasion very publicly as my son Andre was confirmed. During Holy
Mass his younger brother served as an altar boy. We experienced many,
many emotions in anticipation of that sacrament including joy, grateful-
ness, humility, awe, eagerness, and great excitement. The moments were
extraordinarily beautiful and holy.

Have there been times when you experienced deeply personal moments publicly? Is God asking you to live your extraordinary Catholic
faith more fully while sharing your faith in greater measure with your
brothers and sisters?

Almost four years ago I was standing by my computer reading a letter from Priests for Life and was told "I want you to do more." That was
it; no specific instructions were given. Shortly thereafter I began work on
the book that God had placed on my heart about a year or so earlier. I sat
before my computer to get started and asked God, "So what do you want
me to write about?" That first book turned out to be a love story, the story
of how every person has a God-given mission that includes accepting and
sharing the love of God.

*When the Pharisees heard that he had silenced the Sadducees, they
gathered together, and one of them, a lawyer, asked him a question to test
him. "Teacher, which commandment in the law is the greatest?" He said
to him, 'You shall love the Lord your God with all your heart, and with
all your soul, and with all your mind.' This is the greatest and first commandment.*

*And a second is like it: 'You shall love your neighbor as yourself.' On
these two commandments hang all the law and the prophets."* Matthew
22:34-40

Responding to God's promptings can lead us to ask many more questions, especially when we are not given all the specifics at first. Sometimes
those answers come along the way. The most important thing is to recognize the God moments in your life, respond to His promptings, and keep
returning to the Source of Love for guidance, strength, and encouragement.

Every single one of us is God's own. As He lovingly draws us near, He does so privately and also very publicly through very meaningful "God moments." God bless us in our efforts to recognize, accept, return, and share the love of God, which is all encompassing, never ending, and can never be contained.

God is at work in you!

—MICHELE ELENA BONDI

A PRAYER FOR EVERY APOSTOLATE

Prayer for Vocations

Faithful God,
You sent your son, Jesus,
to be our Good Shepherd.
Through our baptism
you blessed us and called us
to follow Jesus who leads us
on the path of life.
Renew in us the desire to remain faithful
to our commitment to serve you and the Church.
Bless all who dedicate their lives to you
through marriage, the single life, the diaconate,
priesthood, and consecrated life.
Give insight to those
who are discerning their vocation.
Send us to proclaim the Good News
of Jesus, our Good Shepherd,
through the power of the Holy Spirit.
Amen.

© 2006 NCCV
www.nccv - vocations.org

CHAPTER ONE

LOVE

COOKING, CREATING, AND COMMENTS

Embracing the world with trusting abandon and love.

My middle child Nick is such a treasure. When he was a baby it seemed he was always happy. Whenever anyone made eye contact with him, my sweet baby would flash them a smile that was so charismatic he melted hearts all over town. As a teenager, Nick's character is developing and his interests are growing, rapidly. He bought a skateboard with his own money and is navigating the ramps at the local skateboard park with greater finesse. He loves nature, science, learning, and helping. He enjoys reading the Bible and teaches the family what he has learned about our awesome Catholic faith.

Nick is a collector and a friend to the animals. Last year he helped our neighbor rescue a skunk. He even helps me around the house. Nick has great ideas; more and more I find myself asking for his valued opinion. Once while barbecuing dinner in the backyard Nick approached me and asked if he could take over. Gratefully I handed over the grill tool (I can't think of the name of it but am sure Nick knows what it is) and we all enjoyed the best barbecued chicken we have ever had. How fun it is to watch him grow.

One morning my children and I went grocery shopping. Nick wandered off a bit and then returned to the cart, delighting me once again with his continuing expansion when he remarked about, of all things, the shish kabob in the meat section. He was very interested in the shish kabob and

3

wanted to buy it and make it for dinner. As he held up the package and awaited my reaction, I looked confidently at the colorful skewered vegetables and meat and remarked to Nick, *"We can make that."* His excitement grew at the prospect of making our own from scratch.

While walking the aisles of the store we discussed ingredients. As the chef he was granted artistic privilege and got to choose the colors of the peppers (he chose green and orange) and to select the vegetables. After lunch Nick and I enjoyed time together as he prepared the meat, vegetables, and the marinade while I offered some suggestions. He was so proud and content and even happier because we took pictures.

Some of his comments:

"I like to cook. It is quite fun and yet difficult at the same time. I enjoy the feel of food in my hands and like to see how my food is made. I like to see what types of seeds are in every type of vegetable and fruit. I also like to cook on the grill because I enjoy watching the food get made and I sometimes like to smoke it."

"I like to work with meats because they cook well. I like to put on spices and I like to see what types of vegetables go with which types of meat. I also feel it is like creating art, because the food is your creation and it takes skill to do it."

Children provide us with such joy because they are curious about the world and delight in the process of discovery. They love so easily. They love us, they love each other, they love the world, they love toys, they love doing things, they love touching things, they love God. Children embrace the world with trusting abandon.

May we embrace our days with a sense of wonder, discovery, and love as children do. God accomplishes much through children, and delights in accomplishing much through us adults. One final quote from Nick's shish kabob adventure:

"I really enjoy cooking just like I really enjoy doing my part in this beautiful world."

—MICHELE ELENA BONDI

RETHINKING THE HARDY DANDELION

A thriving metaphor for God's love.

"Why then did God create a world? God created the world for something like the same reason that we find it hard to keep a secret! Good things are hard to keep...The rose is good, and tells its secret in perfume. The sun is good, and tells its secret in light and heat. Man is good, and tells the secret of his goodness in the language of thought. But God is infinitely good and therefore infinitely loving. Why therefore could not He by a free impulsion of His love let love overflow and bring new worlds into being? God could not keep, as it were, the secret of His love, and the telling of it was creation."[1] —Fulton J. Sheen

Flowers seem to get more beautiful as I get older. Imagine being there to witness the moment when God lovingly created all the many flowers, in all their striking colors, varieties, and combinations. Yellow daffodils. The red rose. A white lily. Pink impatiens. A purple iris. Then, in His infinite generosity, He added white, yellow, and coral varieties to the rose, and pink and yellow to the lily. Impatiens were transformed by the divine brush stroke to purple, white, and red. During spring in Michigan, the trees and bushes erupt in flowers of red, pink, coral, and snow white. The sight and the smells are heavenly.

Where I live, my wonderful neighbors do a great job creating beautiful flower gardens in their yards that emanate extraordinary color. They take great care and work hard so their lawns are well manicured, green, and beautiful. While my flower gardens are in fine shape, my lawn is different from all the others. For a short time every spring, I have the only yard that is dotted with a multitude of yellow flowers. Truthfully they are dandelions, and dandelions are weeds.

I am a huge fan of dandelions, for they are the perfect metaphor for God's love. Even the name is a metaphor for God. The powerful lion is king of the jungle. God is King of all Kings. The dandelion is one powerful plant, while God is one powerful Creator. We humans do not always place great value on the dandelion and work hard to get rid of them, but the plant keeps emerging year after year. Sometimes we do this with God when we do not place enough value on our relationship with Him, but He keeps up His loving pursuit of us. Oh the Majesty, if only we would notice! The dandelion can never be fully contained and is very resilient, just like God's love.

If dandelions could somehow be contained, I would create lovely gardens all over my yard in different patterns of bright yellow. That is impossible, so instead of spreading dandelions all over my community, I will spread the love of God, which is even more beautiful. I will create gardens full of joy, inspiration, and kindness, bordered with gladness, compassion, and mercy. Love will make the gardens spectacular, and the seeds will spread with every gesture, every word, every good intention, every good deed that comes to fruition, and will create more stunning gardens every place I go.

—MICHELE ELENA BONDI

1 Fulton J. Sheen, *The Divine Romance* (New York: Alba House, 1996), pp. 31-32

In Humble Service, We Learn Simplicity. In Simplicity, We Know God.

"Remember that nothing is small in the eyes of God. Do all that you do with love." —St. Therese of Lisieux

As a preteen fiction author, I enjoy speaking to Catholic schools about *Olivia and the Little Way* and how St. Therese inspires me to write. Truly my spiritual sister, she prays for me all of the time. As many times as I've done interviews and presentations, I still get a bit nervous right before it's time for me to go on. During this time, I always send up prayers to the Little Flower, asking her to intercede on my behalf and to help me to spread the message of her Little Way of serving God to youths.

In the beginning of my presentation, I always talk about the life of St. Therese, including her childhood. Therese was a bit of a loner in school, and didn't really fit in with the rest of the girls. They teased her and called her names because they thought she was too smart for her own good, and they were tired of her always knowing the answers when the nuns would call on her. So she spent her recess time by herself while the other girls played sports. Therese would wander off by herself and spend time alone with nature. In my speech, I mention that Therese was a sensitive child, that she had a big heart for all of God's creatures, and so when she'd find little birds that had died, she'd give them her own Christian burial. Hearing this for the first time made me smile, because in our house, we do the same thing when our pet goldfish die, burying them out in the backyard with a little prayer. This is what Therese did when she found dead birds.

One afternoon, after talking about St. Therese and *Olivia and the Little Way* for about 45 minutes, I opened the presentation up to questions from the audience. I had covered a lot of material by this time: her childhood, her spirituality, her entrance into the Carmelite convent, her Little Way of serving God, and her influence on me and illustrator Sandy Casali LewAllen when working on the book.

All of the children's questions were well thought out and interesting, but one question stood out for me. A shy little girl raised her hand tentatively. I called on her. "Um...when Therese buried the birds...did she... um...bury any other dead animals too?" I had to stifle a giggle. It was just so *cute!* After all of the factual information I had given the students during that presentation, the one thing that stood out in this girl's mind was the fact that sweet Therese used to care for dead creatures she had found at recess. It must have really struck a chord with her. But I admit I did not know how to answer her.

Then I remembered that St. Therese had written: "The nearer one gets to God, the simpler one becomes." Little Therese, even at a very young age, was very close to God. In her simplicity and trust in God, she taught us in her Little Way of serving God that it doesn't have to be something big or fancy; simply doing what you do out of *love* pleases God most. He doesn't expect flawless perfection or grand acts of charity. Here this Doctor of the Church, who preferred people to call her "Little Therese," is teaching us not complicated, complex theology, but loving God in all that you do, right down to the simplest thing: caring for God's creatures anonymously.

I held my microphone for a moment and looked out into a sea of young, questioning faces. But my beloved St. Therese, who is with me all of the time, was not going to lead me this far without her heavenly assistance. As always, she pulled me through. "Well, I am not sure, but judging by what we know about Therese, and how thoughtful and kind she was, I would venture to say that she probably would have buried other creatures, had she found them. In her littleness, she loved all of God's creation and I think she would have had compassion for all of His animals."

The girl smiled, satisfied, and I moved on to other questions. But all evening long, I couldn't get that little girl's question out of my head. She had recognized an act of kindness and love. And, of course, we know that Therese was all about love, wasn't she? After all, she once wrote excitedly, "I saw that all vocations are summed up in love and that love is all in all, embracing every time and place because it is eternal...I have at last found my vocation; *it is love!*"[2]

If that is what this little girl takes away from my presentation, the vision of an act of love from the saint who *personifies* love, then I am one happy author!

> —**Nancy Carabio Belanger** is the author of the award-winning novel, *Olivia and the Little Way*. She is a wife and a mother of two sons and is currently working on the book's sequel, *Olivia's Gift*. She enjoys sharing her great love for St. Therese of Lisieux and believes Therese's Little Way is a reminder that we can all make little sacrifices to please God. She writes a blog at nancybelanger.blogspot.com and her website is www.littleflowerbook.com.

---

2 St. Therese of Lisieux, *The Story of a Soul* (Rockford, IL: Tan Books and Publishers, 1997), p. 199.

GOD'S LOVE IS ALL AROUND US

How Jesus Comes to Me.

Sometimes He comes to me as a cool breeze
Knowing how I relish sleeping by an open window,
And waking in the morning as cool air streams in
He gently brushes against my face as I slumber.

Sometimes He comes to me as a ray of light
in the early morning before the day begins,
His love filtered through the multitude of leaves,
immeasurable beams sieved upon the world.

Sometimes He comes through the laughter of my children,
eager for adventure, playfully preparing for the day.
Sometimes He comes to me through the things that I need
to perform the duties along the path He and I have chosen.

Sometimes He comes to me through the delicious food
that nurtures me as I move through each rapid day.
Often He comes to me in the work of my apostolate
and is my strength, offering joy in return for my obedience.

Sometimes He comes to me on the way to Mass,
and always in many diverse ways in His house;
through the music, the homily, and His devoted people.
How many times He has touched my heart so tenderly!

11

Always He comes to me in the Eucharist,
always I know that He is there.
Always He loves me, always He guides me,
always He hopes to find me waiting.

Always He comes at the time
and the place of His choosing.
Always He comes so peacefully,
always He finds that my heart is His.

Jesus, may I spend my life adoring You!

—MICHELE ELENA BONDI

Copyright © 2009 Joseph Karl Publishing

An Unscripted Moment with God on the Bay

His ways are charming and beautiful.

One of my favorite places to visit is Traverse City, Michigan. I love to sit on the beach overlooking the peaceful and serene bay. During the long Michigan winters I take short mental escapes and lounge on the sand while enjoying the beautiful view. The experience is so relaxing, therapeutic, reinvigorating, and inspiring.

Last summer my family spent a delightful week on the West Bay in Traverse City. We left on a Monday and arrived late in the afternoon. My anticipation to be by the water grew during the four-hour drive. After dinner we spent some time relaxing on the lovely beach while the kids played happily in the sand. Then we moved to the indoor pool and played there until it closed. I so longed for more time on the beach!

My plan was to wake up early the next morning before anyone else and relish some time alone by the water. Unfortunately, I overslept. As the family headed to the breakfast room, my disappointment was evident. We enjoyed a delicious breakfast and a fantastic day at the Sleeping Bear Sand Dunes National Lakeshore. After dinner and a lot more fun at the indoor pool, the kids settled in to watch a movie in our room while my mother rested next door. My sister and I decided to sit outside by the water. Darkness had fallen and the beach was peaceful and serene. Such bliss! After a few minutes my sister and I decided to remain outside longer, so we went to our rooms briefly to get something to read. When we returned to the beach, it was pouring rain! I could feel my heart breaking as we went back inside.

The next morning I awoke before the family and, after pouring a cup of coffee, headed for the beach. It was raining. I got a chair from outside, dried it, and set it up in the small vestibule leading from the hotel out to the beach. I was determined to enjoy the bay, not despite the weather, but whatever the weather. Good thing that was my mindset because I was being drawn to the bay for a reason. I was being enticed to faith in the vestibule of the hotel on a rainy vacation day.

This was not the sunny view of my mind's pleasant wanderings, but the view was amazing nevertheless. I was given the opportunity to see the bay as God created it. Nothing made by man was in the water. Some whimsical ducks swam along instead, creating wakes like the absent boats normally would. The sight was so charming. No one was on the beach because of the rain. God orchestrated some time alone with me in one of my favorite places. My God, how generous You are with me. How You entice me to faith. How You love me so!

My beloved Father, I recognize Your Presence in the wonderful world You created and am so grateful for Your Presence within my soul. I am humbled and thankful for the opportunity to witness during our time at the beach that what You created is good. You are the reason the bay is such a special place and You are the reason I long to spend time there.

God, me, and the bay. As I relished being together with God for that private, peaceful, precious moment, lightning flashed in the sky like a strobe light. God, did You have our picture taken? What a special vacation photo for my mind's eye—He and I at the beach on the bay.

So many gifts, so freely given. Let us acknowledge His Presence, accept His invitation, love Him in return, and share His gifts with those around us.

—MICHELE ELENA BONDI

Loving God Like Little Children Love Us

What I learned while volunteering in the cafeteria at school.

Several times during the previous school year I helped during lunch at my children's school. The two-hour shift involved distributing meals through the lunch times of fourth through eighth grades. My fourth-grade daughter was the first of my children to have lunch. After fulfilling my duties I sat with Alyssa at her table. She demonstrated clear outward signs that she was glad to see me. She leaned against me and was happy to have me kiss her head and talk to her and her friends. We cuddled until it was time for me to return to my duties. I returned to work a very happy mother.

When my sixth grader saw me during his lunch he gladly approached me and gave me a big hug. I joyfully hugged him back, and joined him later at his table later where I chatted happily with him and his friends. Once again I happily returned to my duties. Through all the different lunch times, I delighted in greeting and working among the many wonderful children that my children have known since kindergarten.

The time came for my eighth-grade son to have his lunch, and when he saw me he cautiously and reservedly but kindly greeted me. I waved to him and smiled. My heart rejoiced at how blessed my family was to know so many wonderful children and their caring families who were so abundantly blessed spiritually and materially. We have been the beneficiaries of many gifts from God that have been given to us so freely. I marveled while talking with my son and his friends, looking up and down the rows of tables at children whom we had known since first grade. They have grown up so much! So many familiar faces, so much goodness, so much promise, so many people accomplishing so much good for God's glory.

While we chatted, I put my hands on my son's shoulders, something I have done many times before. The jovial atmosphere disappeared in an instant as my son peeled my hands off his shoulders, half turned to me, and said firmly *"Bye,* Mom." At that moment I felt very deeply two distinct emotions. I understood exactly where he was at developmentally, respected his feelings by smiling to him and his peers, and without missing a beat offered a cheery "Goodbye." Returning to the kitchen I struggled with the other emotion, which was very strong and took me completely by surprise: I felt like I had been struck right across my face.

My son had not intended to hurt me while communicating to me that he wanted his space. My reaction caused me to think about what had happened and what it meant. This was another teaching moment for me, and after giving the matter some thought became aware that I do the same thing to God. As I contemplated the mystery of God's immense goodness, mercy, and love for every one of us, I came to see the lunchtime experience as a metaphor for the way we respond to God. We are the children and He is the Parent. Sometimes we respond to God enthusiastically and sometimes we do not.

How *does* God feel when He desires to be with us and we respond, sometimes in front of others, *"Bye*, God"? Perhaps we think to ourselves, "Not now" or "Not in front of my friends" or "I do not want to be out of my comfort zone" or "What will other people think?" Does God feel rejected, slighted, or hurt like I did when I was so glad to see my son and he wanted me to go away? Perhaps we reject God without even realizing it.

Imagine that God is so mighty and always wants what is best for us, yet obediently takes the place we have designated for Him. He allows us to make choices for ourselves. Our Creator has such great love for each one of us that He is subservient to *our* wills while always remaining close to us, always longing and waiting for us to unite our wills with His. We would be wise to honor His wishes. Dear Lord, may I never cause you to feel rejected by the choices that I make!

Let us respond to God like little children in a lunchroom, by showing Him that we are overjoyed to be in His Presence through big smiles, spiritual hugs, and laughter. Let us be happy to be with Him when we are with others and proud to be His children. What powerful witness, what great love!

—MICHELE ELENA BONDI

OUR UNIQUE LOVE STORY

United In Love with Jesus.

Jesus, I long to bestow upon You such great kindness
(for You loved me first and so tenderly),
and rejoice in our exchange of Your unconditional love,
which cannot be contained and extends into eternity.

I greet You with the Sign of the Cross,
love's Captive truly present for us in the tabernacle.
My heart hastens to You and extends a joyful embrace
having missed You, and so grateful to be with You.

As I kneel and pay homage to Your Majesty,
consider the words of my prayers endless kisses
that I delightfully splash across Your Most Holy Face,
humbled at Your longing to be united with me.

While reflecting upon the unique love story,
of the willing Captive of Love and His creation,
may the decision to accept Your love set You free
to unite with me in my heart—Jesus, come with me!

Please absolve me of my sins and abide in me,
that the world may see not Your daughter but only You,
and throughout every moment of every day,
project Your love and invitation to everyone we meet.

—MICHELE ELENA BONDI

Copyright © 2009 Joseph Karl Publishing

EVERY PERSON HAS AN
APOSTOLATE OF LOVE

How the apostolate of St. Therese impacts our own.

D uring preparation for the Sacrament of Confirmation in ninth grade I went through a time of discernment to determine my patron saint. Having no idea who to choose, I properly asked God for inspiration. The word "rose" kept coming to mind. Assuming there to be a St. Rose, I discovered that to be true and concluded, "St. Rose must be my intended patron." However, the decision did not feel right so I asked for more inspiration.

Shortly thereafter, I learned of a French Carmelite nun named St. Therese of Lisieux, or St. Therese of the Child Jesus. She promised to continue her apostolate from Heaven after her death, declaring, "I will let fall a shower of roses." She responds to prayers for her intercession by sending roses as a sign. Once I learned of her I found myself drawn to her in a very supernatural way and was certain that she was to be my patron saint. On the glorious day of my confirmation, St. Therese became my patron saint and friend in heaven.

Like she has done with countless others around the world, St. Therese has touched my life in many ways since. In the weeks before my father died, the scent of roses filled the air and I knew that a great trial was near. Years later I asked her to send yellow roses as a sign that my greatly anticipated first child was on his way. Shortly after receiving a birthday card with a dozen yellow roses on the front, it was confirmed that I was expecting my first son. When Andre made his First Communion, he wore a yellow boutonniere on his suit to honor her. To this day, yellow roses symbolize life and joy to us.

Years later I received multiple signs from St. Therese and knew something very significant was going to happen. All through that great trial I was greatly comforted by the knowledge that she was present along with God to help, guide, sustain, and love me. As she promised, St. Therese was continuing her apostolate of love from Heaven. What great love and mercy God shows to us through His people, including the saints!

What consolation to know that we have such a special ally in Heaven in St. Therese. As she said, *"Everything conspires for the good of each individual soul, just as the march of the seasons is designed to make the most insignificant daisy unfold its petals on the day appointed for it."*[3]

—MICHELE ELENA BONDI

---

3 Rev. John F. Russell, O. Carm., *The Path to Spiritual Maturity: St. Therese of Lisieux* (Niagara Falls, Ontario, Canada: Society of the Little Flower, www.littleflower. org), p. 1.

CHAPTER TWO

DISCERNMENT

THE DECISION MADE AT THE FORK IN THE ROAD

The road not taken.

I n August, 2009 I traveled to Toledo, Ohio to take part in the movie *Leonie!* The film tells the life story of Leonie Martin, the sister of St. Therese of Lisieux. My three children auditioned for the movie that spring. I had no intention of auditioning but a kind woman standing outside the audition room encouraged me to try out for a part. My daughter was cast as Leonie's eight-year-old sister Marie and was in Scene #5 where her little sister Helene passes into eternal life. I was cast as Visitation Sister #2 and put in three scenes.

What a tremendous experience to be a part of the making of this movie. I am always forever transformed in some way by movies on the lives of the saints. The cast met on a Thursday morning at Gesu Church in Toledo, Ohio where we put on actual habits loaned to us by the Visitation Sisters. Later that morning we were transported the short distance from the church to the monastery to film Scene #49. In that scene the choir nuns sing Leonie's favorite song and she drops her book.

25

Entering the Monastery of the Visitation was an incredible experience. After turning a corner I was delighted to see a life-sized statue of St. Therese, my patron saint and friend in Heaven. I felt very close to her in the cloistered convent and we shared a special moment as I passed by, dressed in a habit and participating in the making of a movie on the life of her beloved sister.

How deeply moving it was to recognize God working so powerfully and beautifully in our lives, and how much good each of us can accomplish when we allow Him to work in us. There are so many opportunities and countless ways to serve Him and each other during our lifetimes. The length is irrelevant, as we see in the life of St. Therese, who lived a mere 24 years. What matters is what we do with the time we are given as we respond to God's summons with great love and obedience.

As I walked farther down the hall I passed a large statue of Jesus crucified. What made that experience so meaningful personally was that Jesus was very close to the ground, near me. He remains with us. Great was the feeling of being loved and valued as I walked down that hallway, dressed as a Bride of Christ!

Continuing down the corridor I had an experience that was totally unexpected and astounding. Often I have told the story of how as a teenager I recognized the presence of God in my soul and asked Him if He wanted me to be a nun. His answer was "No." I felt in some way rejected by God, as in my mind the highest calling I could have had would have been to be His bride. Sometimes I lamented to God that if He had said "Yes" I would have been spared the tremendous suffering resulting from my divorce.

At that very moment while walking down the hall of the Visitation Monastery at the age of 44, dressed in a habit and cast as a nun in a movie, it was revealed to me clearly that by responding to God's "No" and instead choosing the path He intended for me from all eternity, *my life played out as it was meant to.* God created me to be a mother. Perhaps this understanding was granted to me as I once again stand at a fork in the road. Perhaps He is saying, "Follow Me as you did before."

I was greatly pleased by having the opportunity to wear the habit and experience the immense love of God present in the convent that had attracted me so many years ago. Continuing down the hallway I came to the final conclusion that while I would have made a wonderful nun, I make an even better mother.

There are so many options available to us as we journey through our lives, so many forks in the road, so many decisions to make. Our efforts at greater intimacy with the divine help us communicate with Him and understand His will for us as we discern. May we remain obedient to Him and give whatever we do our best.

—MICHELE ELENA BONDI

The Soul's Journey

My soul is restless from its birth
Longing for God in my search.
Running along a winding course
Eagerly looking for the Source.

My soul is parched, thirsty and dry
In the dark night of soul I cry;
"My God, my God, forsake me never,
Hide my soul in Your Heart forever."

My soul hungers and burns with desire
For love of God is Divine Fire.
Searing my soul in dying embers
Dying to self, my soul surrenders.

My God, the journey seems so long,
I am weak, yet You are strong.
Clothe my soul in graces sweet
Bring my soul to rest at Your Feet.[4]

—LINDA J. PERAKIS

---

4 Linda J. Perakis, *Led by the Holy Spirit* (Deckerville, MI: Pine Cone Press, 2004), p. 54. Reprinted with permission.

What We Need to Keep On Living

Your presence and participation are lovingly requested.

When I was a child, my father had a friend named Jack. Jack had a great love for God and even considered becoming a priest. He decided to marry and had five children. Jack and my father served together as Boy Scout leaders and also in various capacities at the Catholic church where they met and became fast friends. Dad died several years later but Mom continued to see Jack and his wife in church. Many years later after the children had grown, my mother saw his wife in church one day and she was alone. After Mass my mother spoke to her and inquired about Jack. Apparently he disagreed with someone or something and had stopped attending Mass.

The year 2007 marked the 25th anniversary of my father's passing into eternal life. I felt his presence very strongly through that year. And so it came to pass that God sent Dad to work through us as His instruments of mercy and send a divine invitation to Jack. One Saturday my children and I went to visit my mother and sister. At lunchtime my sister and I went to the local pizza place in a small strip mall to pick up lunch. There was hardly anyone around, but as we left with our pizza in hand, we ran right into Jack.

I had not seen him in 25 years. We talked for a while, and then the Holy Spirit prompted my sister to ask him about his absence from the sacraments. He smiled. He said a few words describing his position. Then I heard myself saying, "The Eucharist always remains the same." He smiled a knowing smile and acknowledged that the Eucharist always remains the same. Dad's dear friend had been summoned to return to Mass. I am certain that my father orchestrated the whole event from his close proximity to God in Heaven. Yes, the saints do intercede for us!

And so at my father's prompting, that year I launched a personal prayer campaign for Jack and all those who have stopped receiving Jesus in the Blessed Sacrament for whatever reason. That campaign continues to this day, and I also pray for myself, for who but God knows what lies ahead. Human nature left to its own devices is weak and vulnerable to temptation. May we never give in to the temptation to leave our strength, our courage, our love, our compassion, our hope, our faith, our joy, our life!

Please pray for me, for yourself, for the ones you love, for those who have left the sacraments for any reason, and for all of humanity. Remember this prayer in your intentions every single day. Know that I pray for you.

—MICHELE ELENA BONDI

"Come Back to Me"

God is in loving pursuit of every person.

While attending college as a young adult I decided to stop attending Mass on Sundays and chose instead to work the weekend hours required of my job in retail. I justified my decision intellectually because it made logical and fiscal sense. My plan was to attend Mass regularly again after earning my degree. However, every Sunday when it was time for Mass and I was at work instead, I felt sad. I did not feel right because I was not in church. That "right" feeling is our God-given internal regulator to help us discern His will for us. I felt God lovingly pursuing me and I wanted to be with Him in His house. I wanted to receive Jesus in the Blessed Sacrament. I missed Him. I needed Him!

One weekday I returned home very tired after a busy morning of classes and took a nap. Upon awakening, I heard the words **"I am all you need to know."** God was talking and I was ready to listen. He pointed out that my priorities were out of order. Shortly thereafter I visited the church where I made my First Communion as a child. Next to the altar hung a huge banner that read "Come back to me." God was still pursuing me! I knew for certain that God wanted me to put Him first in my life, before my education and my job, and return to Mass.

Our most loving God was courting me. I was being drawn to faith. God left the decision up to me. However, it was crystal clear what He wanted! I decided to follow God's will, and made the changes necessary to put God first and attend Mass again regularly. That was one of the best decisions I ever made!

Little did I know then that God's pursuit of me would continue and that one day I would not only be attending daily Mass, but would also receive the Sacrament of Reconciliation regularly. Attending daily Mass was never even a consideration of mine until the day eight years ago when God gently and lovingly invited me to attend. He does not want our relationship with Him to be superficial. The blessings that have resulted from my choices have been abundant. I love to reflect on how God continued to patiently pursue me because of His great love for me. Most compassionate, loving God, I love you back!

—MICHELE ELENA BONDI

THE LEAKY WASHING MACHINE AND THE SURRENDER

Sometimes we are meant to just let go.

A nyone with children in the house never wants to experience what happened to my family. Our washing machine began leaking during the rinse cycle of the first load of wash on laundry day. Immense gratitude for the luxury of having had a working washer preceded the first stages of grieving. The machine was turned off and the soaked laundry wrung out by hand. Piles of dirty clothes sat on the floor. A repair company was called and an appointment for service was made. I was convinced that we could survive for a few days until the washer was fixed. However, God had other plans.

The serviceman came, the repair was not made, and the customer service department was the most unhelpful I had ever encountered. Within a week I transformed into a frustrated, irate, and immensely unsatisfied customer. When all was said and done, the washer remained broken *for weeks*. Nothing I tried improved the situation. At first, I only saw the opportunity to straighten out an incompetent appliance repair company. God saw the opportunity to point out an important character flaw of mine.

The serviceman told me during the initial visit that the part needed to fix the leak had to be ordered, so he made an appointment to return in 10 days. *Ten days?* I was overjoyed to learn that the machine could still be used in the meantime; I just had to mop up the leaking water. I very gratefully paid and thanked the man, and then he left.

Laundering commenced immediately, only to discover that the man had not completely restored the washer after taking it apart to diagnose the genesis of the leak. Now the leaking machine also failed to spin and rinse. Once again I found myself removing soaked clothes and wringing them out by hand. The next morning after daily Mass I got in my vehicle and called the repair company. I notified them about what had transpired and kindly requested that the serviceman be sent back to the house to restore the machine to the condition it was in before he arrived to fix it, so I could do laundry. The woman flat-out denied my request. "I'm sorry," she cavalierly replied. "We can't send out the same person. *It doesn't work that way.*"

"Absurd," I responded, after trying unsuccessfully to reason with the woman. More non-compliance followed. I explained, requested, and rationalized. Then I ordered and demanded. "Send someone. Send anyone."

She repeatedly replied with great calm, "I can't help you." I asked for the manager. She told me there was no manager! I requested my money back so I could hire someone else to come out and *fix my washing machine.* She said she could not do that. So right there on church grounds, with the windows of my car open, I began yelling at the woman. Not screaming mind you, but I raised my voice. She serenely denied every plea.

I contacted the company again the next day hoping to get someone reasonable, but got nowhere. The entire experience seemed unreal. After refusing to pay a second company to come out and do the job, I finally surrendered and decided to make peace with the circumstances. I let go and let God finish the story.

In the end, God helped me understand how hard I am willing to fight for something that really is not that important. He taught me to look for His Hand in situations that require time to resolve and to be very, very grateful for the luxury of a working washing machine. His gifts to us are many, are tangible and intangible, and include luxuries as well as what seems like a disaster. Often times resistance has less to do with frustrating circumstances and more to do with pride and a need to be in control. Fortunately I eventually became aware of the great grace that I had been given. I still smile on laundry days when I reminisce about what God taught me through a leaky washing machine.

—MICHELE ELENA BONDI

Happy 10th Birthday, Alyssa Maria!

God's masterpiece of creation and planning.

When our boys were very small, my husband and I decided to build a new home. Tremendous amounts of time and physical labor went into the building process. We had faith that our efforts would bring our family a lifetime of joy. In contrast, putting time and effort into our relationship with God and seeking to do His will yields an eternity of joy. Such long-lasting benefits are definitely worth working for!

Oftentimes we are surprised, disappointed, angered, frustrated, or sometimes pleasantly surprised; more often we are stunned and devastated when things do not work out according to our plans despite our efforts and good intentions. The unexpected events that occurred during the building of our home provide an example of the contrast of laboring for that which is of this world versus laboring for that which is eternal. Before our house was completed, we discovered that we were expecting our third child. We would have preferred that our home be finished before having another baby, but were open to life. At that time we were in our early thirties and, in my mind, we still had plenty of time to have more children.

This baby seemed to be arriving too early. I had my plan and God had His plan. God's plan was better! The happy family living in the beautiful home was not to be. Shortly after we moved in, the marriage that was to be forever ended and our home went up for sale. So many hopes and dreams were shattered at the same time. Two years later the home we worked so hard to build was sold to someone who sought to take advantage of our sorrowful situation.

In fact, so many people appeared on the scene to take advantage of us that it was reminiscent of Christ's Passion. Many times my feelings of despair were great, but God in His unfathomable mercy chose that very time to send me a child who has been one of my greatest consolations. She and her brothers constantly bring joy and meaning to my life. Praise God that I trusted in His ways more than my own! With the benefit of hindsight I can clearly see God's loving Hand not only in my pregnancy but also in the timing of this child.

One day while still living in the house, the profound loss inherent in the death of my marriage was so great that I cried the entire day except for the one hour I managed to stop while my children and I attended Mass. That afternoon my two-year-old Alyssa had a very special message for me. Somehow that tiny girl found me in my walk-in closet, sobbing. She looked right into my eyes and joyfully said, "Mommy, Jesus loves you!" I knew that God was loving me through her and I was greatly comforted. I love to reflect on the story of my daughter's life. God knew that despite my hopes my marriage was ending and He sent me a wonderful parting gift: my beloved Alyssa!

Years later I realized that I was being tempted during a time of great change to doubt God, His timing, and the very existence of this child. What seemed like a mistake in timing was no mistake at all. She was a case of divine intervention! God saw that her arrival was then or never. He knew that a time of tremendous suffering had already begun for me and sent His servant the very special gift of someone extraordinary.

As I do every day, but especially on the occasion of my Princess Pixie Fairy's 10th birthday, I thank God for creating Alyssa and for choosing me to be her mother. She is so loving, joyful, spiritual, helpful, and beautiful. God is at work in her!

—Michele Elena Bondi

I SAW A TRUCK TODAY

Taking steps to defend life.

First I heard the beeps; I turned my head and noticed a large, white truck backing up into the parking lot. My attention was drawn to the maneuvering of the truck into the gates it was trying to fit between. Then I looked at the name on the truck and froze. You see, I was in front of an abortion clinic. My daughter, her friend, and I had been there for several hours doing sidewalk counseling. We had been standing at a site that was the last line of defense for what I would estimate to be about 25 unborn babies.

We were about to leave for the day when that truck pulled in. The truck broke my heart. It was from a medical waste company and was there to pick up the unwanted CHILDREN! I cannot express the despair I felt. I knew what was going on in there. I knew the different types of procedures used and how the children could feel the pain. I knew that there is even a market for body parts and tissues obtained from LEGALIZED abortions. My heart took in the information, and the only remaining feeling was one of complete despair. I went to my knees and quietly moaned, "No, no, no." Then I said quietly, "My Jesus, mercy!"

Sidewalk counseling is simply a presence in front of abortion clinics in order to get an opportunity to speak to the women for a moment. Counselors are there to give hope to a woman who has none. It is an opportunity to save a baby from the horror of abortion and the child's mother from psychological pain. Women drove in with the God-given blessing of new life within them and drove back out empty. I don't think they were capable of thinking about how that child would be disposed of, or even for a moment fathom the horror: the horror that the child endured, the horror of the disposal site, the horror they would probably endure for their entire lives. This is the horror I felt when I saw the truck.

I cannot stop abortion or be any more effective at sidewalk counseling. I can continue to try though, and it all begins and ends with God, just as each person's life does. I turn to God and pray for the end of abortion and a renewal of the respect for human dignity at all stages of life.

I read years ago that St. Faustina would ask our Lord for huge favors. He could not deny her because they were always for the benefit of others and He loved that she knew how big her prayers could be. I always remember this when I am offering up a somewhat unpleasant task. I used to do gardening for a friend at her dog kennel in order to help pay for my precious dog Cuddles' boarding. I spent many long hours pulling weeds. So I asked Jesus to save a soul for each weed I picked. It felt great to know that even little things like that could help others and help my relationship with God grow stronger.

Well, here I am many years later with an unused treadmill convicting me to finally get started exercising again. Year after year I got started only to stop the routine. One day I had the idea to ask God to save a baby from abortion with every step I take. My first time lasted only a few minutes, but my time is increasing. As I walk, I think of more things to ask—the release of a soul from purgatory with each step, one healing, one conversion, one job, one home for a homeless person...the possibilities are endless and I BELIEVE these prayers are being answered! I couldn't ever seem to exercise for some reason when it was for my own good, but now I have a newfound purpose. TRY IT—WE CAN TAKE STEPS FOR LIFE!

—SHARON ROSE CECIL

What Do You Do When God Calls You?
You respond to His summons

"We should say every morning: 'My God, send me thy Holy
Spirit to teach me what I am and what thou art!'"[5]
—St. John Vianney

One Sunday morning my children and I were having breakfast
before departing for Holy Mass. That Sunday morning was very
different from any other one in our family's history. Midway
through our meal I could not contain my many emotions any longer and
started crying.

We have shared many diverse experiences together, my children and
I, including joyful moments and also tremendous suffering. Every single
day has become for us a great adventure. That particular morning their
young eyes focused on me with great wonder. What had happened? What
happened is that our lives had changed forever. Again!

I did my best to explain despite being overcome by so many emotions including profound humility, immense gratitude, uncertainty, and
joy mixed with sadness. The children already knew part of the story, how
I was driving to daily Mass through downtown Rochester one morning

after dropping them off at their schools and was instructed to take my two youngest out of their Catholic school. By that Sunday morning, Nick was already attending a different school. They also knew that I was told to take them to a specific parish for Holy Mass on Sundays.

That very morning we were to attend our first Sunday Mass there. We had already joined the parish, met with the pastor, and felt very welcomed. When it came time to decide about religious education, I explained to Father that we had been called to that parish for Sunday Mass but I had not been given additional instructions.

As a single parent and the only driver in the family, with our new parish twice as far as our other one, and with three children in three different schools, I was worried with the prospect of life getting even more challenging with this new summons. I was still processing everything that happened and it was all happening so quickly! I was unsure at that time if we were to leave our current parish, and the thought of leaving the church so dear to me, as well as our many wonderful friends there, made me very sad.

God, being so loving and compassionate, already began laying the groundwork for our transition the year before. That was of great comfort to us as we followed His lead. We had already met some parishioners the previous year during auditions and rehearsals for the movie *Leonie!*, which were held at the church. We also know parishioners from our other parish who go to Mass there on weekends.

When Father stated that Catechism was on the same night at the same time for all three children, and it was not their visitation night with their dad, I shared a smile with Father, acknowledging that God had everything worked out all along. Did He leave some things a mystery to me to test my faith? Dear God, I do trust in You and we did what You asked because we love You and reverence Your judgment.

Recently my children attended Catechism at our new parish for the first time. Eucharistic Exposition and Adoration is held on the same day as religious instruction. The children are taken from their classes to the church for Adoration and remain through Benediction. An unexpected joy is that while my children attend Catechism, I get to spend time before the Blessed Sacrament in the church or more privately in the chapel!

After my children met their instructors their classes started and I went into the church to spend time with Jesus during Adoration. There are no words to describe what I experienced upon entering the church. Jesus' presence was so striking, so incredibly beautiful, and all encompassing. I had never experienced anything like it, ever. I cried the entire time I remained in the church and knew for sure that we were called there with good reason. As Benediction ended I went out into the hallway where my children were told to meet me. The doors of the church opened and more altar boys than could be quickly counted processed out of the church. They all genuflected and Father led them in prayer. What a beautiful, beautiful moment that was! I wish you could have seen it. I cried all the way home and for the rest of the evening. Incredible. Incredible!!

And so that Sunday morning at breakfast the children were told something they had not heard yet. I had not intended to tell them at that time, but felt they needed to know that I was not crying because I was sad—I was very deeply touched and filled with great joy. When I was instructed to take them to Holy Mass on Sundays at our new church, I came to know one more thing: Someone in our family will be called to the priesthood.

I explained to my children that I was not told who God would call or when. Who, from what generation, and how many remain unknown to us. Certainly our summons will benefit each of us as individuals. The benefits will also resonate among us and extend to all our brothers and sisters, for we are all interconnected. While our individual formation is of immeasurable importance, the vocation to the priesthood was of particular significance with regard to our summons. Our cooperation is necessary.

Several weeks after I received our summons, we were in a Catholic store when a man came in. We were introduced, and as God would have it, I already knew who he was. I had met his mother during rehearsals for the movie *Leonie!* Deacon Jim has very special ties to our new parish. In May he is going to be ordained to the priesthood. He asked what parish we belonged to, and without explaining anything else I told him that we had been summoned to attend Sunday Mass at a specific church. He responded that belonging to that parish and speaking to Fr. Ben were instrumental in recognizing his call to the priesthood. We parted ways acknowledging that indeed, that had been another very significant "God moment!"

This past Sunday my sons Andre and Nick served as altar boys for the first time at our new parish. It was Nick's 13th birthday. My daughter Alyssa and I sat in the church and as Mass started, the double doors opened and we could see the altar boys processing in, so many of them, from very little to very big. What a powerful moment! Again it was evident that we are being prepared for something(s) to come. I am still processing the events and can testify to you that God has plans for every single one of us. For this reason, every life is to be defended. Everyone is loved, every life has value, every person matters.

"To do things well, one must do them as God wishes."[6]

—St. John Vianney

—MICHELE ELENA BONDI

5 Compiled and Arranged by W.M.B., *Thoughts of The Cure' D'Ars* (Rockford, IL: Tan Books and Publishers, 1967), p. 49.

6 Compiled and Arranged by W.M.B., *Thoughts of The Cure' D'Ars* (Rockford, IL: Tan Books and Publishers, 1967), p. 34.

CHAPTER THREE

FAITH

THE NEIGHBORHOOD
HOCKEY NET

A boy on a bike saw true value in it.

Two years ago our neighbors were cleaning out their garage and decided to get rid of the big red hockey net that the previous owners had left behind when they moved out several years before. My neighbor asked us if we wanted the net. I was reluctant to bring another item into our lives, but my children saw potential in the big net. So I reluctantly agreed. Later on, my children rarely used the net and I grew tired of looking at the big thing sitting idle in the yard. One day I encouraged my boys to bring the net out to the curb, hoping that someone would come by and take it. The three of us labored to get the large net to the side of the road.

We left to run an errand and on the way out passed the red goal covered with rust spots, the net discolored through the years and ripped in several places. I told the boys that if no one took the net, they were going to have to dismantle it so we could throw it in the trash. No one was looking forward to that job! Later upon our return, we noticed a boy who had been riding his bicycle stopped on the side of the road in front of our net. He was staring at it with wonder. As we pulled into our driveway I stopped the car by the curb and rolled down the window. The sight of the boy looking at the hockey net was so delightful.

Almost sure of what he would say, I asked him, "Would you like to have the net?" He was overjoyed! I was overjoyed that he was going to take the net away from my property. I even offered to put the net in my van and deliver it to his house. He declined my offer, never taking his eyes off the net. He was so thrilled to take possession of the goal he rode home on his bike, walked back with a friend, and the two boys jubilantly carried the heavy net down the street to his house.

I smile every time I think of the boy on his bike at the curb, seeing such a prized possession in the beat-up net. Don't you just love to see the expression on children's faces when you tell them they can have what they ask for? What a thrill it was for him to take possession of the net so easily. Riding one's bike down the street, one never knows what one may find. What an adventure this life is!

Our faith is a lot like that hockey net. We use it and enjoy it during times of leisure. Sometimes we fail to see value in our faith until someone comes along who greatly prizes it and sees it for the treasure that it really is. It does not matter if it is not brand new or if it is imperfect. Faith always has value. Our Father is so happy to grant our request to have it, and is filled with joy when we see value in having faith.

Yesterday we looked down the street and saw the boy happily playing hockey with the net in his driveway. What a wonderful sight to see him enjoying the net for the treasure that it is.

—MICHELE ELENA BONDI

THE EVOLVING APOSTOLATE

The end of some dreams led us to even better realities.

This week has been quite a week in my evolving apostolate. Last weekend I made a decision, and Monday was trash day, the day my plan would come to fruition. I climbed up into the storage space above my garage and brought down a very heavy storage container. After placing the container on the driveway I lifted the lid for the first time in over seven years. I took one last look at the contents and then carried the container to the curb.

As I poured the contents into the recycle bin, I was reminded of all that was left undisturbed in my attic all those years. Inside of the container were many thoroughly read research articles, outlines, correspondences, ideas, forms, papers, revisions, and a final dissertation proposal. There were also a few pictures and notes reminding me of the many facets of my apostolate all those years ago. Professional. Wife. Mother. Ph.D. candidate. So many memories tumbled out of that container, and I was ready.

Some history: Before my children were born I began working on a Ph.D. in psychology. I already had a masters degree and was eager to complete my doctorate and focus on my greatly anticipated apostolate of motherhood. After all the other requirements were complete I began work on my dissertation, but encountered major resistance from my advisor. The resistance continued and so eventually I switched advisors. However, my former advisor was a permanent member of my committee and his resistance continued. He created extra tasks not required of others that seemed impossible to execute. I completed every one.

Finally, I presented my dissertation proposal and it was accepted. That afternoon my advisor called to inform me that there had been personal infighting within my committee and several members reversed their decision to accept my work. At that moment I was unjustifiably stopped from obtaining my Ph.D. Even with a justifiable reason, I still had a one-year grace period left to complete the final requirement to everyone's satisfaction. When I brought that to the attention of my department, the grace period was denied me as well, and no formal reason was ever given for either decision.

When all was said and done, I was denied the doctorate I had earned because several members of the department did not like one another. While I had heard of this happening before, I never thought that would happen to me. After years of study, the cost of tuition, having passed first-year exams, having earned a scholarship, having passed written and oral qualifying exams, and having completed my dissertation proposal, the unthinkable had happened! I was in shock, I was angry, but mostly I was extremely frustrated.

Certainly the unfairness was very difficult to take. The university's ombudsman said there was nothing he could do. Not only had plans years in the making abruptly changed, but I was terribly wronged in the process. Despite my best efforts, things had not worked out the way I had planned. One day the Holy Spirit inspired my sister to tell me that the only possible explanation was that for some reason, God had allowed the injustice. Finally, a reasonable explanation! As it turned out, my sister was right.

A month after receiving the final word regarding my degree, I received divorce papers in the mail. At that time, so many of my dreams ended abruptly and traumatically. As time went on it seemed that things went from horrible to worse to even more terrible. Denied my degree. Death of my marriage. House for sale in a tough post-9/11 market. Future uncertain. I had five needles stuck in my neck to determine if I had thyroid cancer. The results were inconclusive. I cried a river.

Even when I had no guarantee of what the future would hold, even when I did not feel like it (which was often), I clung to my trust in Jesus like a life preserver. Just as Jesus' Crucifixion was followed by His glorious Resurrection, my suffering led to great good. I was granted the tremendous grace of an unwavering faith and constant trust in God through many bleak moments. Nevertheless, the pain was very real. God did not take away my pain and for good reason, for it was during my trials that I experienced tremendous spiritual and personal growth that I know would not otherwise have been possible. God was always present—loving, comforting, helping, teaching, and guiding me. *We are so much closer today, He and I!*

During those brutally painful years, God very tenderly beckoned me into a deeper personal relationship with Him. At that time I received God's gentle, loving invitation to attend daily Mass, and shortly after that to receive His Precious Blood. Note that His most profound invitations did not come when things in my life were going well. Through frequent reception of the Eucharist, regular Reconciliation, Eucharistic Adoration, and prayer, God provided me the strength to get through each day, grieve, forgive, consider a different path, become excited about the future, recapture joy, and embrace my evolving apostolate.

How crucial it is to remember not to discard our faith when we need God the most! We must persevere and not abandon Him during trials, for He remains with us and He has important plans for us. Each of us is necessary in His plan of salvation.

One particularly difficult day, I went into church to pray about my continuing hardships, and immediately heard, *"Your prayers are working."* That revelation from our compassionate God who shared my pain helped me to continue trusting in Him and to remain faithful. While it took years for me to see great proof through my eyes that my prayers were working, the work was indeed in progress and God clearly manifested Himself in countless delightful ways. We must remember that God knows and sees things that we do not. Through it all, He has taken very good care of us, especially when we needed Him the most.

There at the curb that Monday, I had resolved to throw the entire contents of the container out and keep nothing, but I changed my mind while staring into the recycle bin. I removed a few forms and my final dissertation proposal, and praised myself for a job well done as I tucked the papers into my work file. I prided myself on letting go of an old dream while accruing recycling points in the process. The many papers were very heavy!

My recycle points will go toward a gift card at Panera Bread, an important part of my wonderful apostolate. There I enjoy the delicious hazelnut coffee while writing and editing. I greet friends and learn there, share, gather new ideas, and work on books. I have also met many new people there and together we have shared fellowship, a love for God, kindness, and lots of laughs. Letting go of my doctor dreams freed me to do the work I am meant to accomplish. I work for God, started a business at His command, and the world is my office.

My apostolate evolved not in spite of or despite my trials but because of them. I am most grateful to God for the opportunity to serve Him in the way that He wants. Is your apostolate evolving through difficult and traumatic circumstances? Always remember that God is the source of your strength and your guide. Keep trusting. Allow your apostolate to evolve. Pray!! God has a plan for your life, and your life is necessary in His plan of salvation. Encourage others in need of hope.

"...Today, if you hear his voice, do not harden your hearts..."
Hebrews 3:15

—MICHELE ELENA BONDI

THE SHEPHERD

The shepherd searches for His sheep,
Some of whom are sound asleep.
Some of them have lost their way,
Some have even lost their faith.

He gently knocks on every door,
Waits patiently, then knocks some more.
Lord, it is my sincere request,
That You're more than just a passing guest;

And it would mean to me a lot,
If You're more than just a passing thought.
That in every heart You'll find a home,
And bless it to its cornerstone.

A home that will have a welcome gate,
That opens to a place of faith,
And a hearth that burns with love,
In an ambiance of peace and trust.

With windows that look within,
With prudence and reflection;
And curtains that windows dress,
In tidy rooms that are clean and modest.

Where are woven tapestries,
Of scenes of selfless charity;
Where mirrors bear silent witness,
To faces lit with holy purpose.

Lord, it is my sincere request,
That You're more than just a passing guest.
That in every heart opens a door,
So You can enter and live forevermore.

—BELINDA BONDI

Copyright © 2010 Belinda Bondi

How the Lord Drew Me Near: One Catholic's Reflections

"God is spirit, and those who worship Him must worship in spirit and truth." John 4:24

One of the things I have learned, as the Lord opened my heart to the Love of the Father, is that the true worship of the Father necessarily involves entering into a living relationship with Him. Without such a relationship we can only approach worship from a distance as from the outer courts of the Temple. The true worship the Father desires of us is through a loving relationship with Him—a relationship that may only be realized through a relationship with Jesus, in whom the fullness of the Godhead resides.

As a (more or less) traditional and cultural Catholic, I was observant of all the church rules, partook of the sacraments and attended Mass regularly, and assumed that my attendance at Mass was *de facto* worship. The beauty and reverence of the services did help me to reverence God, His Word, and the sacrifice of His Son that brings us to salvation and acceptance as His children. I also believed that during the Mass (the Catholic Eucharistic service) I was a participant in that awesome and magnificent act of God's love for humanity and that, by being present, I was in fact

present at the greatest act of worship ever. However, my personal participation in that worship was limited in that I perceived myself more as a
devoted observer than a participant.

One circumstance that limited me was my lack of spiritual awareness through faith. At the intellectual level, I assented theologically to the
concept of the Mass being a participation in Christ's offering of Himself
to the Father, but in hindsight, I know now that I was not entering the
level of awareness of being in communion with Christ during the worship
that I ought to have had. I cannot speak for others, but for me, before my
conversion experience, I never really comprehended the full meaning of
that worship in my spirit. Metaphorically speaking, it was as if I were an
observer of the Temple worship from the court of the Gentiles, but never
as an actual participant in that worship in the Holy of Holies as I ought to
have been. For that reason I could not, at that period in my life, say I had
personally experienced, at the spirit level, the worship that the Father desires, which is that we worship Him "in Spirit and in Truth." Now, I must
be clear, I did also believe that I received the Body and Blood of Christ
at the reception of the Eucharist and I can say that the sustenance of the
life of Christ did help me through some difficult times in my life. I am
only attempting to state that there was a certain dullness in my spirit that
prevented me from receiving the fullness of the graces that flow from the
sacrament of His love. It was only after my conversion, which opened me
to a spiritual awareness, that I have been able to experience the fullness
of the worship at Mass, the Eucharistic celebration.

As I later discovered, through the grace and inspiration of the Holy
Spirit, there were three major factors casting a veil over my worship.
These were as follows: (1) my spiritual ignorance, (2) my un-yielded self-
will, and (3) the hidden sins of my heart.

SPIRITUAL IGNORANCE

"My people are destroyed for lack of knowledge..." Hosea 4:6

My ignorance consisted of not clearly understanding that we humans are endowed by our Creator with three levels of awareness: (a) an awareness through our physical senses of our physical self and the material world around us, (b) an inward mental awareness of our personal identities and all of our intellectual and our emotional attributes and capabilities (i.e., what we sometimes categorize as the "soul"), and (c) the spiritual level of awareness, which we sometimes identify with the human heart or spirit. This latter level of awareness is intuitive, non-conceptual and non-verbal and includes our conscience. It is this latter level of awareness that we sometimes ignore or overlook as a part of our personal assessment. Yet it is at this level of awareness that our Creator intended as the level where He desires to meet with us and establish a personal relationship that brings us into communion with Him. Due to Adam's act of disobedience (original sin), however, this level of communion with the Holy One was disrupted in Adam and all his generations.

I must add with great sadness that my ignorance extended further to the fact that I did not understand that in order for me to connect with the Father in true worship, I had to enter the spiritual level of my spirit, which had been renewed in me through baptism. I also was not aware that, even though baptized, this channel of relationship remained inactive and needed to be activated through an act of my will—by a sincere, heartfelt repentance and conversion. In my traditional and cultural passivity as a young child, I went through the motions required of me in receiving the sacraments but did not truly understand the level of heartfelt repentance and commitment needed in giving my heart to Jesus. As a result, although the graces of baptism and confirmation worked in the circumstances of my life, I had not totally yielded my inner self to my Savior, Jesus, thus creating a veil that kept me from a true relationship with the Lover of my soul. Through the grace and mercy of the Father, the Holy Spirit continued working in the circumstances of my life so that as an adult He brought me to the point where I recognized my need to know Him in a personal way, and thus, after a heartfelt repentance, I turned to Him in a conversion of heart, inviting the Lord Jesus into my Heart and thus beginning a personal relationship with Him "in the Spirit."

MY UNYIELDED SELF-WILL

"Then Jesus told his disciples, 'If any want to become my followers, let them deny themselves and take up their cross and follow me. For those who want to save their life will lose it, and those who lose their life for my sake will find it.'" Matthew 16:24-25

This brings me to the next barrier that hindered me from fully entering the spiritual awareness I needed to truly participate in worship, namely my self-will. You see even though I had come to conversion and repented of my known sins, and turned to the Lord for his forgiveness, I still retained my self-will. That is, I had not fully yielded myself to the Holy One. In my continuing ignorance and of course my pride, it had not entered my mind that what the Father desired of me is the total yielding of myself to His reign in me. I incorrectly supposed that I, in my turning to Him, could now use my self-will to serve Him. So the Holy Spirit had to make it clear to me, through His Word, that I had to deny my self-will in order for the Lord to rule in my life. I had to yoke myself to Jesus so that through that yoking, my desires and my thoughts would become His desires and His thoughts, and thus my actions would be in conformity to His will and thus "walk in the spirit."

Of course, once I understood my problem, I repented again and made the decision to surrender myself completely to His reign in me. What this decision did was to begin a process of transformation in me, that I now continually come to situations where I have to put down my self-will so that He and He alone would reign in me. This tension between my spirit and my flesh is still the cross I have to bear daily, but now I am more aware of my self-will attempting to creep in; by the grace of God, in Him I have the spiritual strength needed to walk in the spirit and not in the flesh. Praised be His Holy Name!

THE HIDDEN SINS OF THE HEART

"Who shall ascend the hill of the LORD? And who shall stand in his holy place? Those who have clean hands and pure hearts, who do not lift up their souls to what is false, and do not swear deceitfully. They will receive blessing from the LORD, and vindication from the God of their salvation. Such is the company of those who seek him, who seek the face of the God of Jacob." Psalm 24:3-6.

Having yielded myself completely to the Lord, He then began His work of transformation in me to conform me more and more into His image. He began His work in me with a very thorough house cleaning. In this process the Holy Spirit began to reveal to me the secrets of my heart.

Although I had repented of my sins at my conversion, there were secret sins that I harbored in my heart that were barriers to the fullness of worship. These were sins that I had long ago buried in my subconscious by justifying them as merely human idiosyncrasies. They were very personal sins, which included things like: bitterness originating from unresolved personal grudges and hurts, an anger and cynicism toward others that came on me for no apparent reason, a prideful and stubborn attitude that always placed my ideas and will above others, and flowing from this sulking behavior when I didn't get my way. These sins affected all my relationships, but again I was blind to them because they were so deeply hidden in my inner self. Even now I still encounter them attempting to creep back into my life, but now that the Lord has brought them into His Light I am rapidly aware of them and bring them under His Blood in confession. Some of these sins are gone forever as the Lord healed me of my inner hurts and I forgave all who had injured me. Praised be His Holy Name!

WORSHIP REVIVED ME

As the Lord worked His transformation in me, my worship experience continued to deepen. In the beginning, after I received the Baptism in the Holy Spirit, I experienced a totally heavenly worship at a Mass conducted after a spiritual retreat. I literally thought I was before the throne of God. I experienced a sense of communion with the Lord that I had never experienced before, a communion that extended to all who were present in the church as well. Now I began to truly understand that the ideal for the fullness of worship is in a corporate setting. There, we believers as the "Body of Christ" in communion with Him are, in fact, also participating in His Priesthood at His ultimate act of worship as He offers Himself to the Father in compliance with His merciful will for the salvation and redemption of humankind!

Later the worship experience spilled over even beyond my participation at Mass to personal worship time with Him. I noticed this happening during the daily events in my life. For instance, sometimes I would enter into worship as I was driving to work and I would have to stop until the experience passed and I was able to drive again. Nowadays, I find myself going into worship during my evening prayer times and when I am exercising in the gym. Thus is the Glory of the Lord manifested in us!

IN CONCLUSION

Like the man born blind who received his sight from the healing Hand of Jesus, and having been given new life in Him, I now wish to tell others (whatever their religious upbringing or lack thereof) who are still seeking, about the renewed spirituality that comes with knowing Jesus personally and the more vibrant worship and prayer life that abounds when you put aside your inhibitions and yield your self to the Spirit of the Living God and receive the Baptism in the Holy Spirit.

To Jesus, our Blessed Savior, be Glory and Honor and Praise forever and ever! Amen!

—GEORGE MADRID SR.

DONATION, REJECTION, AND THE RIGHT RECIPIENT

God's timing is always perfect.

A few years ago while cleaning the garage I made the executive decision to donate some toddler toys my children had outgrown. I loaded the giant toy car, the five-foot basketball hoop, a wonderful train set, and various other things in my van and drove the large lot to a local donation center. When it was my turn I drove up, opened the van door, and happily displayed the toys that were sure to bring other children joy like they had to my children. Instead, I was surprised when my donations were rejected. None of my donations had been turned down before. Curious, I thought. The toys returned home with me that day.

Fortunately my mindset was in full "trust-in-God" mode. The toy donation was unfolding as another example of God having other, better plans. For several weeks I eyeballed the toys in the garage and considered where I could donate them. One day I decided to put everything at the end of my driveway along with a sign that said "free." Throughout the afternoon and evening I kept checking out the window, hoping that someone who could use the items would come by and take them away. Night fell. I was so disappointed at the thought of having to bring everything back into the garage. Then the doorbell rang; a young woman was at the door. God love her, she came to the house to ask for permission to take the toys despite seeing the sign. I think she could not believe that everything was free for the taking!

The young woman explained that her mother had just opened a day-care center and would be thrilled to have those items for the children. God had a plan! I was so happy to share her joy at that moment, so happy for her mother, so happy for the children she was looking after, so grateful for all that my children have been blessed with. What tremendous joy fills my heart to know that God is so intimately involved with the details of our lives and loves us so very much. When we see His Mighty and Loving Hand at work in our lives and cooperate with His plans, we are rewarded with a front-row seat to watch all things work out in His most delightful way.

—MICHELE ELENA BONDI

BLESSINGS ARE ALL AROUND US, LIKE AIR

We just have to realize it.

I have always been a cautious driver. I remember taking driving lessons in high school when I was 16. I was scared and thrilled at the same time. My driving instructor also happened to be my civics teacher. As I had no regard for him in class, him being my driving instructor was not going to be much better. I managed fairly well in driving and passed the course.

Two things always gave me headaches: parallel parking (which to this day I do not do—I will park a mile away before I even attempt it) and left-hand turns. After years of avoiding left-hand turns, I finally found the answer to my problem.

I heard a priest at Mass give a homily about how God gives us all kinds of things to help us deal with life, specifically our guardian angels, and how we don't take advantage of this blessing. God gave us our angels as helpers to deal with the struggles of daily living. I started giving this a great deal of thought. I wanted to be personal with my angel and so I called him Alexander, although Andrew creeps into my thoughts when I want to talk to him.

I ask for his help with a number of things, especially left-hand turns. Upon the approach of a left-hand turn, I now always ask Alexander/Andrew to please clear the traffic for me so that I may continue safely to my destination. The traffic always clears. He has helped me in other daily situations and has always come through.

Remember the prayer we were taught by our mothers: "Angel of God, my guardian dear, to whom God's love commits us here, ever this day be at my side, to light, to guard, to rule, and to guide." In this prayer, God is giving us loving help. We just have to see it for what it is: more blessings from above. God is eternally good and is giving us blessings every day. We just have to realize it.

—LYNN CZAR

"If You Want to Believe in God, Go Ahead!"

Wise words left in the back of a book.

Recently my children and I read together from the book *A Treasury of Miracles for Teens: True Stories of God's Presence Today* by Karen Kingsbury.[7] Each chapter tells an amazing story of how teenagers came to understand that God was present, loving, helping, and guiding them. One story was about a 19-year-old aspiring singer who was invited to join a Christian group that was touring in the southern United States. The group traveled by bus from location to location, bringing God's love to many people through song.

The teen's mother warned her before she left that if her intentions did not focus on serving God while on the tour, she would end up being very disappointed. The girl aspired to be discovered, travel to exciting places, and have luxury accommodations during her time touring with the group. As it turned out, the reality of being part of a small group of Christian singers living in a tour bus that relied on the contributions collected at each church they visited did not provide the lifestyle she had hoped for.

Often the group dined inexpensively at fast-food restaurants, and often the group leader gave money collected for their needs to other people he determined needed the money more than they did. The teen was often disgruntled with her standard of living. Then one day the group received enough money to afford a sit-down dinner. As the teen followed the group toward the restaurant she noticed a beggar standing outside. The group leader invited the man to dine with them and insisted he sit with their group. Guess who he ended up sitting next to? The disappointed teen. All the typical judgments and stereotypes of a person in his situation came to her mind.

Then, right there at the table during the group's discussion with the man, she experienced a complete change of heart and found herself joining the group in sharing the love of God with the beggar. The man was deeply touched by the kindness of the group. During dinner the teen asked God to forgive her hardness of heart. The group offered to take the man to the next town where he would receive assistance, but on their way out they lost sight of the man and did not see him again.

My children and I were very moved by the story, but God was not finished with us yet! While closing the book I noticed something that we had not seen before. Someone had written on several lined pages meant for taking notes at the end of the book. Although the book belonged to the library, the person felt compelled to write in it anyway. We read on with great interest.

This is what we read, exactly as it was written:

"I have a small story I want to add to this book. I am twelve, and I have a hermit crab named Shelly. If you drop a hermit crab for more than 2 feet, they die, most of the time. (I read that on a website). So one day I took Shelly outside on our concrete front porch. And then I acciedently [sic] dropped her and she fell 3 feet at least. My heart was broken. She wasn't dead, yet. But I knew she would die soon. Shelly has been my best friend for a year. I did not want her to die. So I prayed to God to help me. I cried, I prayed, and I felt awful. 5 days passed and you know what? Shelly lived! I was overjoyed! If you want to believe in God, go ahead! Something like this may not happen to you, but God is still watching you. ALWAYS! Read it! Psalm 56:3."

In honor of this insightful, faith-filled child who made it a point to witness what believing in God can accomplish, this is Psalm 56:3: "*... when I am afraid, I put my trust in you.*"

If you want to believe in God, go ahead!

—**MICHELE ELENA BONDI**

---

7 Karen Kingsbury, *A Treasury of Miracles for Teens: True Stories of God's Presence Today* (Warner Faith, 2003).

Can I Just Shake the Package?

God provides for what we need, but sometimes we are required to wait.

Six years ago I felt terrible and needed treatment for an overactive thyroid. Five years ago I needed to move. Three years ago I needed divine intervention. Two years ago I needed a reliable vehicle. Then I needed a computer to write my first book. Last year I started a new company and needed capital. God has always provided for my needs. Now there is something else that I need and I prefer to have it right now. Unfortunately for my human nature God has not deemed it the time, yet. Fortunately for me His plan will be better than mine. Some things never change.

Jesus' arrival had been foretold by the prophets and His people waited in eager anticipation, but no one knew exactly when He would appear. Perhaps many little girls grew up hoping to be chosen as the Mother of God. The Virgin Mary made a vow of chastity to God and, placing herself entirely at the Lord's service, seemingly gave up the possibility of becoming His mother. Yet she is the very one God chose to be His mother, and at the foot of the Cross Jesus declared her as our mother, too. Mary waited and trusted in God, even when His plans seemed impossible.

Throughout our lives, we find ourselves in want or need. Perhaps we strive to attain a personal goal or a new job, want a (or another) child, hope for a holy spouse, need to pay the bills, or desire an answer, intervention, or resolution. We may be discerning what comes next for us, choosing a vocation, getting a pet, embarking on a new career, overcoming loss, planning on taking a trip, starting a business, longing to overcome an addiction or character flaw, finding a place to live, hoping to do well in school, making a good friend, purchasing something we need or want, seeking a cure, or picking up the pieces of our lives and starting all over again. Sometimes things happen or come to us quickly, and sometimes we are meant to wait.

The readings at daily Mass last week focused on the story of Abraham and Sarah. God promised them a son, but given their advanced age Sarah doubted what God said and took matters into her own hands. Her lack of trust in God led to her taking action that ended up causing grief for herself and many other people. God did not stop the actions of her free will, but was always concerned with their greater good. Abraham and Sarah eventually did have a son, Isaac. The story serves as a reminder to trust in God, even when His plans seem preposterous. The trick is discerning when we are to wait patiently and when we are to take action. Our culture teaches us to be self-reliant, and certainly being proactive and active can be a very good thing. When to act, when to wait?

The trouble starts when we lack faith and fail to go to God in prayer and ask Him what He wants. Perhaps we do not want to know His response, or we know what His response will be and want a different outcome. We do not like to wait. Perhaps we convince ourselves that what God has planned is impossible. Perhaps we misunderstood? We get frustrated, but God does not negotiate. Then when our frustration reaches its peak, we return to Him for guidance. So He uses a sweet image to instruct us about the importance of sometimes waiting. We see ourselves in a metaphor as a child repeatedly asking our parent if we can have our birthday present early. "No," He says with a loving smile; we are just going to have to wait!

Our lives are at times a mystery, but God is always there teaching, guiding, loving. Acquiring sanctity involves self-denial as we work to develop behavior that is consistently healthy and holy. Trusting, letting go, and waiting can be difficult. Our life circumstances are the classroom and God is the teacher. We must keep communicating with Him to learn and discern, and be willing to follow His direction if we want to become, as speaker and author Matthew Kelly says, "the best versions of ourselves."

Last night I had a delightful discussion with a dear friend who has had many trials and been in need of many things. As we discussed God's plans for her and for me that require discernment and waiting, I told her about my experience the day before at Reconciliation. The wonderful priest was returning from a wedding in another town and was half an hour late. With 5:00 Mass just around the corner and other people in line, I tried to be very brief and to the point in the confessional. That is what made his comments all the more striking. With little information from me, and very patiently too, he encouraged me to be thankful to God for all that I have been given. While God has me wait for what I want and need, I am to be mindful of how much He loves me and has abundantly blessed me. My dear friend waits in eager anticipation for something as well. She and I shared a hearty laugh when she looked up to heaven and asked, "For now, then, *can't I just shake the package?"*

God is always present throughout our lives and takes pleasure in delighting us while we wait for His perfect timing. Whatever the circumstances are in your own life, keep asking, keep listening, keep trusting, keep loving, keep thanking, keep going, keep finding joy, and if necessary, keep waiting. God is at work in you.

—MICHELE ELENA BONDI

CHAPTER FOUR

HEALING

A Pecan Roll and God's Mercy

"I Could Not Believe What Was Happening to This Little Girl"

Deceased Loved Ones and the Beatific Vision

Ad Majorem Dei Gloriam (For the Greater Glory of God)

The Blood Draw That Had Us Both Shaking

This Was One Journey I Did Not Want to Take

"I Will Bless Them with Many Graces"

"I'm Surrendering, I'm Surrendering!"

A Pecan Roll and God's Mercy

What love God has for every one of us!

While writing my first book I followed a regimen that included dropping my children off at school, attending daily Mass, doing some writing at a local restaurant, and then ice skating before going home to attend to domestic duties. One day, my typical routine was altered because God had something else in mind that morning. When I arrived at the restaurant, my usual spot way in the back was occupied by a large group. So I was led to a corner table more centrally located. I ordered the fruit plate right away but for some inexplicable reason held off ordering whole-wheat toast like I usually did.

Normally I would have worked for about an hour or so before heading to the local rink to exercise. However, recently I had a bad fall on the ice and was avoiding skating while the back of my head healed. So that day I remained at the restaurant and worked longer than usual. After about an hour and a half, having enjoyed several cups of coffee and the fruit plate, I decided to follow a strong and unusual desire to have a cinnamon roll. So I asked the waitress if they were good, and she said that she thought the pecan roll was better.

Being a creature of habit, I hesitated. The waitress indulged me in my dilemma and pointed to the woman sitting with her back to me in the next booth over. I was informed that my neighbor had ordered the pecan roll. My interest was piqued and so I sat up a little taller to see over the woman's shoulder and sneak a peek at the pecan roll. After a short verbal exchange with my very helpful waitress, I confidently ordered the pecan roll.

I can assure you that God has a sense of humor. When the pecan roll was set on my table, the woman in the next booth turned around and stated that I would enjoy it, adding that she was partial to spreading strawberry jam on hers. She passed me her container of jams while I thanked her for the suggestion. Then, after tasting the pecan roll with the jam, I delightedly remarked that it WAS good, and my neighbor turned around again momentarily and gave me a knowing smile. I returned to my work and we did not talk again after that until I got up to leave.

I packed up my laptop computer, papers, and books, and on the way out said goodbye to my neighbor. It was then that she told me that she also had not ordered her standard fare that morning because *she had the same craving I had for something sweet.* Then she asked me about my profession. I went through my standard litany of "mother, writer, psychologist, servant of God" and she responded by telling me that she really needed to talk to someone. She said that when she entered the restaurant she felt compelled to go to the area where I was sitting and sit by me. She followed the urge but did not disturb me while I was working. We made a connection over the pecan roll!

On a normal Monday I would have missed her, but because of my injury at the rink I remained at the restaurant longer than usual. She told me about her personal exodus and we discussed God's providence in all that was taking place. I gave her a Divine Mercy key chain (a daily Mass friend had given me some to give out) and a final revision of *Your Personal Apostolate: Accepting and Sharing the Love of God,* which I just happened to have with me that day. We parted ways in awe at the power of God and His great mercy. How much God loves that woman; how much He loves each one of us!

—MICHELE ELENA BONDI

"I Could Not Believe What Was Happening to This Little Girl"

How could we possibly continue knowing what could happen?

February 27, 1984 is a day that I will never forget. I was working at my office at General Motors when at approximately 10:30 that morning, the phone rang. The caller identified himself as Dr. David, my daughter's pediatrician. I thought to myself, *This is a strange call.* He proceeded to tell me that I should come to his office immediately. I threw on my coat and headed out the door.

Upon my arrival at the doctor's office, the receptionist escorted me to one of the examining offices where I found my wife, Emily, and my four-year-old, Jacqueline, in tears. By then I was trembling, too. The doctor came in, put his hand on my shoulder, and told me the blood test he just took on Jacqueline was positive for A.L.L., Acute Lymphoblastic Leukemia. Stunned in disbelief, I asked him to take another blood test. He assured me that one was all he needed.

He then referred us to a doctor at St. John Hospital in Detroit. This doctor was a pediatric oncologist that dealt with that type of illness. He immediately scheduled us to start a protocol that was being used, requiring chemotherapy and radiation.

We were young parents who had never experienced this type of illness in either of our families. We had to have some direction so we listened to the advice of this doctor. In the meantime he sent us to Harper Hospital in Detroit. The hospital conferred with us and told us the ramifications of what to expect with radiation. Jacqueline was placed on the examining bed as the staff prepared her for a mold that was designed to hold her head in place during the radiation therapy. They drew purple lines on her head, zeroing in on the area they wanted to radiate. Emily and I were in tears throughout all of this.

The mold was made and we were in the process of scheduling the dates that she would be radiated. We went home and waited. All throughout this ordeal, prayers were offered by family, friends, and Jacqueline's classmates. Things looked very bad. We found out that the radiation would most likely affect her learning ability and could cause a host of other potential problems. How could we possibly continue knowing that this could happen?

After returning home Emily spoke with family and friends and someone suggested we take her to William Beaumont Hospital in Royal Oak. Someone she knew was being treated for leukemia there. They were using a new protocol that had been developed at St. Jude Hospital in Memphis, Tennessee. St. Jude is a children's hospital that treats all forms of cancer, so we were encouraged by the information we received. We met with two wonderful doctors at William Beaumont. The chief of pediatric oncology explained the protocol to us. Although no radiation was going to be used, the large doses of chemotherapy would probably cause health problems later in life. Jacqueline was facing five years of treatments.

We went through emotional ups and downs. Jacqueline's immune system was severely depressed. One of the worst illnesses a young person afflicted with leukemia can get is chicken pox, which can be deadly. Sure enough, Jacqueline got chicken pox. The scars are still evident, but by the grace of God she survived another setback.

I couldn't believe what was happening to this little girl. I asked God for His help on more than one occasion. After all, who does one turn to if not to God? I prayed continuously, asking God to please take me and spare her so she could have a normal life. All around us, little boys and girls were stricken with this deadly disease. Unfortunately, many died from leukemia.

After the five-year treatment period ended, we worried about a relapse. Many children relapsed and then had to begin treatment again. It was bad enough going through this once, so we prayed this wouldn't happen to Jacqueline.

Today, 25 years after she was diagnosed, Jacqueline is doing well. By the goodness of God, she graduated from the University of Michigan, met a wonderful young man named Matt and married in August 2005. She is employed by Fox Sports as an account executive. She loves to golf and follow the local sports teams and her beloved University of Michigan Wolverines.

Her mother and I still worry about the consequences of all the chemotherapy and how it will affect her later in life. I still ask God each day to keep her safe and healthy.

God Bless each of you.

—Chris Camilli

Deceased Loved Ones and the Beatific Vision:
Remembering Those Who Have Passed Into Eternal Life

"Blessed are those who mourn, for they will be comforted."
Matthew 5:4

I was in school one day when I was summoned to return home immediately. I remember clearly that my father dropped me off in front of my high school and then went to work. I do not remember what class I was in, who came to deliver the news, or what was said. Upon my arrival home a few minutes later, my mother said that my father was in the hospital downtown and we had to go there right away. I drove the two of us to the emergency room at Detroit Receiving Hospital where my father had been taken after having a massive heart attack at work.

While my mother and I awaited news, my brother was summoned from his class at the university nearby and my sister from her university two hours away. At some point my mother and I were led into "the room." As soon as I saw where we were going, nothing else needed to be said. A kind woman from Dad's office sat with us at the hospital and accompanied us into the room. The three of us sat in the tiny room in shock as we were told that Dad was still alive but would not survive. Dad's co-worker hugged me, and with her act of compassion the floodgates of sorrow were opened.

My brother arrived at some point, and then my sister. A Good Samaritan on a four-hour trip of mercy drove my sister to the hospital and then returned to the university. Everyone was given the news. Dad had been playing cards with a co-worker on his lunch break when he collapsed. The very dedicated emergency room staff worked heroically to save his young life, and kept him alive for the rest of the day and through the night.

I had to see my dad once more while he was still living. I pleaded with my mother and brother to allow me into his room. The very compassionate hospital chaplain helped us with the decision and I was allowed in. The scene was very traumatic. Dad's eyes were open and his arms were moving as if he was resisting; it appeared that he was battling against death and struggling to live. There he was at the threshold of eternity, about to leave his young family behind. To me it seemed like Dad was experiencing for one last time the battle an individual soul wages between the will of God and its own desires. There was a lot to be considered, but God was summoning him and it was his time to go. I remember my mother lovingly rubbing his feet as his life came to a close. She was experiencing the same struggle of acceptance and letting go.

The doctors continued to resuscitate Dad throughout the night. They brought him back only to have his heart fail again. Our hopes and modern science were no match for God's plan, so often a mystery of faith and trust. I remember our small family awaiting the final outcome throughout the night. While we waited, I had the perception that time had completely ceased to exist. Our father was dying, and time no longer had meaning or purpose.

At around six in the morning a doctor came to tell us that Dad had died and we were brought to him to say goodbye. Mom was 40, my brother was 20, my sister was 19, and I was 17. God love the young resident who was there trying to save his life. She grieved, too, and cried right along with us. I'll never forget her.

So I stood over the body of my father who had been separated from us so soon. His health problems began when he suffered a massive heart attack that destroyed a significant portion of his heart at the age of 39. At that time my mother was 33, my brother was 12, my sister was 11, and I was 9.

I remember saying many rosaries as a child with my family on Dad's behalf. I also remember going to St. Bonaventure in Detroit where Venerable Fr. Solanus Casey is buried, the beginning of a life-long friendship with our dear Capuchin ally in Heaven. In fact, more miraculous interventions through Fr. Solanus were to come 20 years down the road.

Dad lived for seven more years after his first brush with death, and that was our miracle. He was an honest, hard-working man who loved his family, loved my mother, and honored his marriage vows. My mother cared for him very heroically through those seven years as they both grew in virtue through their trials. Dad was a true gentleman and lived his life very much like his namesake St. Joseph did. After a life lived in imitation of Christ, the time came when God summoned Dad, and the faithful servant entered into his eternal reward.

Recently I spoke to my sister about the moment when our father died, and asked her what she had experienced in the hospital that morning. I was astounded to have been the only one who witnessed something very extraordinary: I saw my father enter into the Beatific Vision, one of the most beautiful things I have ever seen. Dad was in the presence of God! Oh what heavenly consolation for my grieving soul! My father had suffered greatly the last years of his life and served God so nobly, and when he died he radiated joy the likes of which I have never seen on anyone's face. My father was not dead, he was very much alive, and he was so happy!

We buried Dad near Boston where he grew up, and returned home. Life continued on for us, but the head of our family and source of our income was gone, we missed him, the pain of grieving was tremendous, and the bills kept coming. Even though I knew my father was with God in Heaven, times were tough emotionally and economically after his death. Mom was very valiant. So many of my best traits were acquired through the fine examples of my parents.

The course of my life was altered dramatically by my father's death. I was set to go to Michigan State University after graduation and study journalism. Instead, I remained home with my grieving mother, attended Wayne State University, and by divine providence changed the focus of my studies to psychology. God was present through everything: loving, guiding, healing, encouraging, inspiring, and helping us.

Grieving is normal and necessary as we come to terms and cope with the loss of loved ones as our apostolate evolves. Maria von Trapp of *The Sound of Music* fame told a very inspiring story in her book *Maria: My Own Story*. In the weeks after the death of her husband she went through a time of what she described as terrible struggles. As she relived her married life, she felt terrible about the times she had been unkind to her husband. She wisely sought the counsel of a priest and told him her whole story.

"When I was all through, Father Raphael looked at me so kindly and lovingly, as our Lord must have looked at some of those evil women he cast demons out of. There were very few questions and answers, and then he informed me that this had been a general confession over my whole life and he was now giving me absolution. That meant, he said, that not only God almighty in heaven, but also my dear husband who is now in God and loves me more than ever before, will have forgiven and forgotten all those sins." She returned home at peace and happy, "…to try now—as Father Raphael had admonished me—to undo the past damage by doing good from now on."

A very important point she makes is, "As he is now with God, he is so much more powerful to help me…He is so close to our heavenly Father that one glance will be a supplication."[8]

All those who mourn, be comforted with the knowledge of God's great love for us and His infinite mercy. Know that He has a plan for every one of us that is good. Allow yourself to grieve, forgive, be forgiven, and continue on with the plans God has for your evolving apostolate. Continue to pray for the deceased.

Dad's godfather, Gus, survived my father by many years. He lived in imitation of Christ into his 90s. As he passed into eternal life surrounded by family and friends, he said to everyone, **"See you soon!"** May all those who mourn be comforted during this time of temporary parting, and may the souls of the faithful departed, through the mercy of God, rest in peace.

—MICHELE ELENA BONDI

---

8 Maria von Trapp, *Maria: My Own Story* (Carol Stream, IL: Creation House, 1972), p. 111.

Ad Majorem Dei Gloriam (For the Greater Glory of God)

O Lord, were we going to lose him so soon?

I was due on the 14th of February and the day came and went. I was so full and the baby was so low the entire pregnancy. I said a rash prayer to God, "Lord, let someone who doesn't know I am with child call me and tell me I am going to have this baby." Then I repented of that prayer and said, "I am sorry, Lord. I am just so tired and hurting."

An hour later I received a phone call from a seminarian who did not know I was carrying a baby. He said "I have only a couple of minutes, just listen and take it as you will. I had a vivid dream last night. You are going to have a baby and you will be living in another house. I could even tell you about the layout of the house but I have no time now."

I replied, "Oh Joe, I am overdue."

He said "I have to go. I will be praying for you."

Apparently God answered my prayer. After our conversation I actually felt lighter, as if I could carry this baby as long as our Lord asked me to. Finally on the 20th I went into labor. It was a very uncomfortable labor and seemed to not want to progress. We went into the hospital at about 3:00—the hour of Mercy. I was in labor all night and then labor abruptly stopped at 6:00 a.m. The doctor told me to shower and then took me to a room. He said, "Do whatever you have to do to bring him down, but don't tell me what you have done."

So I did some jumping jacks and squat thrusts and then a man came in the room. I could not continue in front of him. So I just walked in circles and watched this father-to-be. He sat down and put his face in his hands and started to cry. I asked if there was something I could do for him. He said that his wife had been in false labor six times and this time their little one at home said, "Daddy, don't come home without our baby."

His wife said she could not go through that again and her labor just stopped. He said, "We can't do this. We need her to have the baby this time!" I told him not to worry, that I would be praying for them.

I walked back to my room, pulled out the stool from under the bed, and put it next to the bed to use as a kneeler. I prayed "Lord, please let that lady have her baby normal and healthy. You can send me back home if you like. I'll gladly offer it up for her and that family."

At that moment the doctor walked in. You should have seen the look of horror on his face. "Have you fallen?" he asked excitedly.

"Oh, no, Doctor, I was just praying."

"Okay, let's check you. Good—we can have this baby now. Tell your husband to get ready."

In about a half hour I was complete. Ron was sent to get into his scrubs. I was rushed into the delivery room. Ron came in just in time. The doctor said, "Okay, push." I thought, *I don't have it in me. I'm just too tired.* Ron put his hand under my head and grabbed my hand. At that moment I could do anything. I pushed and he crowned and slid into this world.

Ron said, "Is that all?" I could have slapped him.

We had a modified Leboyer method delivery. The lights were turned down as Ron and baby and I bonded in subdued light and quiet music. We were the warmth for each other and just relished in the moment that God had given us a son who lived. Could there ever be a better gift?

Ron had to go to work and I was very tired. They took Ronnie to the nursery to clean him up and dress him. I went to the recovery room; after 36 hours of labor I was ready to sleep. When I got to my room I thought, *Well, Lord, this is my moment to tell of your love. I spoke to my roommate who already knew You and loved You in the same way I do. It was exciting but not what I thought You were leading me to do. So when I was given a student nurse I thought perhaps this gal did not know You well yet. No, wrong again. She knew You and loved You and witnessed to me about You. O Lord,* I thought, *what is going on?*

When I lost my other son Levi Benjamin I was devastated. My heart was in shreds, my arms ached, my mind questioned whether I was not good enough to bring him into this world.

Why, why, why, Lord? We needed a son. I thought you were going to give us a priest for our family. After months of sadness and depression I asked for another son. Like Samuel's mother, Hannah, I said I would give him back if I could just hold him for a little while, but I thought a little while would be years.

I was waiting for the nurse to bring Ronnie in to nurse; he had not done well four hours before. The nurse came in and said they could not bring him in at this time. I have forgotten what her excuse was, but I was told that if I was patient the doctor would be in to talk to me.

The day shift came on and my student came in. The next thing I knew the doctor walked in and said, "Your son is in the intensive care nursery. We don't know why but his heart is racing and his oxygen level is low. He is in an incubator on oxygen and we have him on a broad spectrum antibiotic. You will not be able to nurse him and you and your husband will have to scrub and suit up to be near him."

O Lord, am I going to lose him so soon? I wondered. At that moment the doctor left and my roommate grabbed my left hand and the student nurse grabbed my right hand and they prayed for me, our son, the doctors, all who would be working on him, and especially that our Lord and Blessed Mother would be with us all and heal this baby. The

Lord was showing me that He already had me surrounded with His love and protection, before I even knew I needed it.

My mind was swimming. *What am I to do, how am I to respond now?* I called Ron and told him that our son was in intensive care. He said he would come right back in. I asked him to call Ss. Peter and Paul Church to let them know we needed prayer and anointing. I had been in labor so long I filled up with fluid. When I looked at myself in the mirror I did not even seem myself. When Father Larry came in to anoint me he did not even recognize me. He turned to leave, thinking he was in the wrong room. I had to call him back. He apologized but said I looked different. "Yes, Father. I know," I said. He anointed me.

Ron came in and we scrubbed up and put on the surgical clothing. Ron did not want the baby to be named after him, but after 36 hours of labor, he gave in. So there was little Ronnie, all covered in leads reading out all kinds of data: Heart rate, pulse, oxygen level. Our son was like a pet in a little isolette cage. My poor husband; his heart stopped, seeing his boy in there.

What were we to do but touch him and speak to him, as his eyes were taped shut so that the oxygen would not destroy his eyes. The only senses our dear son could use in this situation were hearing and touch. We were going to stimulate them so that he would not lose them. He could hear we were with him and we loved him. Sometimes I thought, *I am petting him like a cat but he needs to know I am here.* I leaned over the incubator and prayed into his ear. "Our Father who art in Heaven, hallowed be Thy name, Thy kingdom come, Thy will be done, on Earth as it is in Heaven. Give us this day our daily bread and forgive us our trespasses as we forgive those who trespass against us, and lead us not into temptation but deliver us from evil. Amen."

A.M.D.G.

Ronnie was using a pacifier since he was not allowed at breast at that time. His suck was not strong because he was having a hard time breathing. They were feeding him by nasal gastric tube that went through his nose and into his stomach. I wanted to feed him but on the first day they did not even want me to get out of bed. So I would go back to my room and pray, and the next hour go back for another 10 minutes or longer if no one said anything to me.

On the second shift the nurse took out the preemie NG tube and tried to stimulate Ronnie to nurse. He did pretty well; at least he swallowed some. The nurse on the third shift did not have the time to sit there and feed him, so she put another NG tube in and it was not a premature size, so he was really hurting. I was very upset that they would not allow me to feed him, because I had time on my hands and I am his mommy.

Ron came in early the next morning. We scrubbed up and I was telling him about the nurse putting a child NG tube in Ronnie and how that upset me and hurt him. As we were walking into the nursery, Jean, a nurse I used to work with, said, "You'll never believe this. Your son pulled his NG tube out, balloon and all intact."

"I guess he didn't want it," I replied.

I was then given permission to feed him every four hours, no matter how long it would take. Yessssss! The bad news was that someone forgot to give him the pacifier, so he forgot how to suck. I couldn't believe it. *What else can happen?* I thought. *Oh, don't ask, Susan.*

O Lord and Blessed Mother, what am I to do for this son of mine? THIS SON OF YOURS! I shouted in my heart. Prayers were being said for this baby in Shreveport, Louisiana; Seattle, Washington; Salisbury, Maryland; in Steubenville, Ohio, where the seminarian lived, and in Hamburg, New York, where we lived.

With all this prayer, it seemed that everything was going from bad to worse. I went back to the nursery and the nurse said, "You have to be extremely careful of this IV. It is the last one we can place, as all of his other veins have blown. We have to finish his antibiotic."

So that ordeal began. I would go into the nursery and carefully extract him with all his wires and the IV in tow. Then with a little value feeder bottle in hand, I gently pushed his chin up to squeeze milk into his mouth.

Most frightening was that instead of swallowing, which I thought he would do, he just let the milk drool out and we would begin again. Sometimes I thought he got some so I would strip him and weigh him. Alas, nothing. It would take hours to get only one or two ounces into this baby.

One shift would leave and another would come on and I would still be there trying to feed this son of ours, the treasure we prayed so long and hard for. A son after his father's own heart.

Ron took my mom back home and after a little rest and prayer I went back into the nursery. The nurse looked at me and said, "This baby is losing weight and he only weighed 5 pounds 10 ounces at birth anyway."

I said, "Well, all he needs is to have his mother hold him and he will improve."

A.M.D.G.

It was the night shift. I was so tired. That day they tried to make me go home without our baby, but I said, "I will stay in the waiting room day and night if you will not let me remain with him." The doctor said I was still in pretty bad shape so he could authorize that I stay in the hospital for a few more days.

Our small daughters Sandra and Trisha had not seen me or the baby and were begging Grandma and Daddy to be allowed to come and see us. They had their classmates and the whole school praying for us. Sandra had made us a beautiful card and Trisha wrote us a scriptural note.

It was from 1 Samuel (16:7): *But the Lord said to Samuel: "Do not judge from his appearance or from his lofty stature, because I have rejected him. Not as man sees does God see, because man sees the appearance but the Lord looks into the heart."*

Trisha said, "Do not worry, Mommy. Man looks on the countenance of man but GOD looks on the heart. God has our baby's heart in His hands." She did not know that I prayed Hannah's prayer for this baby.

The nurse gave me a rocking chair that seemed to keep little Ronnie awake while I pushed his little chin up and tried not to give him a bed sore. It was turning so red. I prayed. I begged. "Lord, what am I not doing that You want me to do? I trust You."

"Sing psalms and hymns" was the answer.

At first all I could think of, was "Row, Row, Row Your Boat." My mind was so in need of sleep. That is not a hymn nor a psalm. I remembered the hymn by Dan Schutte based on Isaiah: "I the Lord of Sea and Sky. I have heard my people cry. Who will bear my light to them whom shall I send? Here I am, Lord. Is it I, Lord? I have heard you calling in the night. I will go, Lord if you lead me. I will hold your people in my heart."

Then I sang Carey Landry's "Hail Mary, full of grace, the Lord is with you. Blessed are you among women, and blessed the fruit of your womb, Jesus. Holy Mary, Mother of God, pray for us sinners now and at the hour of death." And something happened! As I sang he sucked, held, and swallowed. I had never realized that swallowing had three steps before. One, suck; two, hold in the mouth; and then three, swallow.

This little baby had just taught his mommy something. I was so excited I just could not stop singing. I was afraid if I stopped he would forget again. I asked the nurse for another bottle and weighed him, and—thank You, Lord—he had taken two ounces in a matter of minutes. I put him back in the bassinet and got some sleep. I woke up about 7:00 and called Ron. "Honey, you have to come. No, don't be worried, I have wonderful news." He came in a rush. I told him it was wonderful news and not to look so scared. We scrubbed as I said baby Ronnie was no longer in the isolette, although we still had to take precautions.

I picked up our little baby boy and with bottle in hand I started to sing. As he was rocked in my arms we watched him suck and hold and swallow. "THANK YOU LORD!" Ron said. Then he asked if he could feed Ronnie. This was the first time he was allowed to hold his son since he was with him in the delivery room. That was such a wonderful sight. Our hearts were full of joy!

Then we started to have trouble putting the nipple in his mouth because he would not take it. We would try and he would scream. I said,

"Oh no, we were making progress, what is wrong now?" The doctor came in and told us Ronnie had thrush and his mouth was just full of it. Gentian violet would fix the problem. He was ready for his first dose, so we thought we would watch while the nurse gave it to him. She had a busy nursery. She went to baby number one, changed him, washed her hands; went to baby Ronnie, gave him the med, washed her hands. Then she went to baby number three, changed that little one, washed her hands again, and returned to Ronnie to change him. As she touched him to remove his diaper, he spit purple medicine all over. She was so startled she started to laugh. I had forgotten to tell her he knew how to hold fluid in his mouth.

The whole family was watching: Sandra, Trisha, Grandma and Grandpa, and Daddy and me. We all laughed and that was the comic relief we had needed for days. Finally, after eight days and nights, we were going home. I was on complete bed rest but I didn't care. Our son was well and we were taking him home with us. I was so excited.

We got home and took only one trip up the stairs to our bedroom. I was under strict orders not to take the stairs again until the doctor said I was well enough. Sleep was so wonderful. Just to be able to turn over and pick up our son from his little hamper right next to the bed and nurse him was awesome. Such a gift. I would read him Scriptures and sing him songs.

Every day someone would come in our house, either a neighbor, cousin, or someone from church, and call up the stairs, "I'm here to fix you breakfast, lunch, or dinner!" They were all so kind to us. My young cousin Lisa would come after school just to look at the baby and visit. Sometimes she would even change a diaper. I really enjoyed her visits.

The strange thing was that the people who brought presents for Ronnie were all men. Men don't usually come to give a child presents; it is the women or the wives, in my experience. That is when I realized that our Lord has a special plan for this baby. May he find his way to the Lord's plan and become the great saint God has called him to be.

—ANONYMOUS

THE BLOOD DRAW THAT HAD US BOTH SHAKING

God holds the record for best job performance.

I had my blood drawn during a routine physical. As the young medical assistant entered the room, I found myself trying to redirect my attention away from the discomfort radiating from her. "How are your veins?" she asked nervously, increasing my apprehension.

I battled back with an optimistic reply. "I have great veins. You are going to LOVE my veins."

The assistant looked around the small room with uncertainty and finally decided to have me sit in a low chair beside the exam table. My arm was to be placed across the table for stability. Apprehensively I complied while wondering about having blood extracted in this unfamiliar position. She dropped the needle, collection tube, and tubing on the table next to my hand. The objects used to help me maintain good health now seemed like instruments for my impending torture. As the young woman placed the rubber tourniquet around my arm, she timidly voiced her dislike for drawing the blood of other people.

She picked up the implements. "It's a small needle," she said, perhaps with the hope of comforting both of us.

Confidence fully eroded, I replied, "There is no such thing as a small

91

needle." So there we were, two very reluctant people on a mission to obtain my blood, with me on the short end of the stick. I looked away as she positioned the needle, and gave myself a quick pep talk. "She must be new at this and that's okay. Everyone has to start somewhere." I was ready to sacrifice myself for her progress.

And so my glance returned to my arm as her hands made their way the short distance to my helpless vein, which was hopefully large enough to contribute to a happy ending. The young woman's hands were shaking—significantly. And so, with no confidence left to lose, my arm began shaking, too. There was still enough time to work myself up into a small panic, but with no way out I opted to resign myself to pain and bruising from what was sure to be the absolute worst blood draw ever.

When all was said and done a short time later, I joyfully praised the assistant for the best blood draw I ever had. There was not even the slightest pinch as the shaking needle entered and exited my shaking arm (my son joked that we must have been shaking in unison). The assistant concluded with a confession that despite her loathing for drawing blood, she was the one left to the job while the regular medical assistant was away at lunch. So we both survived, and I am most grateful to the kindhearted woman who for my sake went ahead and did something that was very unpleasant to her.

Not knowing the outcome of the situation in advance, I was quite nervous about how things were going to play out. Fortunately for each of us, we have a very loving and generous God that constantly seeks our greater good. He is not new at the job, nor is He the substitute for someone else. Most importantly, He cares for us consistently, willingly, and with tremendous love.

We may shake with anticipation, worry, and panic at the situations in our lives, but God never wavers. Put your trust in Him, for no matter what your circumstances, God will get you through. Also speak often to others about your faith in God and encourage them to be confident, too.

—MICHELE ELENA BONDI

THIS WAS ONE JOURNEY I DID NOT WANT TO TAKE

How the events of my life led me closer to God.

Being a cradle Catholic, religion has always been a part of my life. My spirituality was always there. I don't know how; perhaps it was my awesome second-grade religion teacher or our family praying the rosary together on our knees, or because my mother named me after St. Teresa. I wanted a relationship with God. In high school I would attend morning Mass before school. Although I was the only teen among the elderly parishioners that attended Mass, it was a wonderful way to start the day.

I can't explain my need for wanting to be at Mass, even though I felt that I did not fit in with the widows or did not understand why more teens wouldn't want to start their day at Mass. In junior high our class received our confirmation from Archbishop Joseph Bernardin; I was so thrilled to be confirmed by the Archbishop. I was aware that the kids in my class did not share my elation. One Lenten season during high school I prayed the rosary using *The Scriptural Rosary* book. There was a deepening in my relationship with God that I still feel today.

The first big decision I had to make in my life was where to attend college. I was the oldest and first in the family to attend college, so there

93

was not much guidance for me. In my prayer I would go out to a newly developed park and sit with my Bible. I would ask God to put me on the right path that would lead me to the right college. My best friend asked me to go along with her on a college visit to the University of Dayton. I did not know anything about the school, except that it was expensive since it was a private school. On the tour I saw the school library was called Roesch Library, which got my attention, since my last name was Droesch. I felt God was telling me to take a serious look at UD and I did. I spent four wonderful years at UD and met my husband there.

During my life, specific events have brought me closer to God. One such event happened when I was 25. The last weekend in February both my grandfathers passed away. It was a difficult weekend of crying and mourning. Learning of my paternal grandfather's death at the viewing of my maternal grandfather was overwhelming, but then to see my grandmothers embrace at my paternal grandfather's viewing was devastating. Their combined grief was so painful for me to see. Through all the sadness I came to know the resurrected Christ in my heart. Jesus came to my heart and took the pain I had and revealed the joy of the Resurrection.

During my life there have been times when my prayer life was stronger than other times. During one particular time, I was praying to conceive a second child. There had been many unsuccessful tries and a miscarriage. I asked the Lord if I was going to only be blessed with one child. At the time I was reading *The Daily Guidepost*. One day the daily reading was about a mother whose daughter had tried and tried and finally had a girl named Elizabeth. This was my sign, since we had picked out the name Elizabeth if we would have a girl. Although a girl was unlikely in my husband's family that had three generations of boys, I became pregnant and delivered a girl! We named her Elizabeth.

At 38 I was diagnosed with stage III breast cancer. I was given a journey I did not want to take. Our family had moved the year before to a state where we knew no one, and I had an eight-year-old son and a one-year-old daughter. This was a crushing blow that became a curse and a blessing. The year of treatment was hell. The support of family, friends, and strangers was uplifting. My son's new school asked parents to provide us with meals and breast cancer survivors would come up to me just to give me encouragement. My prayer life was a mess. I couldn't pray "Your will be done" because I was so afraid the answer would be to take me to Him. It was such a struggle to pray. For most of that year I just visualized myself in the "Footprints in the Sand" poem. God was carrying me through this journey. During my radiation treatment and MRI scans I prayed the Hail Mary over and over to calm my fears. She was there mothering me, so I would be able to mother my children. When the year of treatment was done I was physically, mentally, and spiritually drained. I had to start developing my relationship with the Lord.

—TERESA KOEMPEL

"I Will Bless Them with Many Graces"

Venerating the Divine Mercy Image.

In September 2009 I was running into my sister's house when I hit a rise at the entrance of the garage floor. I fell on my face, full force on my knees, and especially on my right leg. My right leg swelled up to the point that I could not bend it. It was *very* painful. I didn't go to the doctor because I thought, *Oh, I fell other times and in a couple days or so I was okay.* But this time I was in constant pain for three days and three nights. I had absolutely no sleep during those three days because of the pain.

I have a Divine Mercy image on my kitchen table. That image is special. The image was acquired from the front cover of a church bulletin. The frame is also special. I found the frame in my kindling wood box. My nephew, who specializes in woodworking, had said, "Burn these, they are not perfect." I saw this one particular frame in the pile and put it on the side 10 years ago. It just lay there all that time with the other kindling wood. When I needed a frame for my Divine Mercy image, my eyes caught a glimpse of that frame. I stained it and put the image in it. Yes, it does look beautiful.

After my garage accident, I needed help for my knee and leg, which was all swollen. I thought, *The Image!* I took the Divine Mercy image, tied it against my leg, laid down on the couch, and fell asleep. I woke up after about three hours. Cautiously, I put my leg on the floor and was able to walk as if nothing ever happened. I think Jesus healed my leg because I do venerate that image.

After all, Jesus said to Sister Faustina, "Whoever venerates this image, I will bless them with many graces."

—LUCY

"I'm Surrendering, I'm Surrendering!"

No health concerns escape His knowledge.

One Saturday morning in August 2009 I felt fluid in my left ear and predicted a problem was imminent. Later I ended up in urgent care and received antibiotics for an inner-ear infection. Weeks later I was still not well and so, hoping to find a family practice doctor closer to my home, confidently called the office of the physician that had been so highly recommended. The woman on the phone informed me he was no longer accepting new patients.

Naturally I had hoped that things would go smoother but I immediately looked up to heaven with the phone pressed against my bad ear and silently asked God to direct me to a good doctor. Then I asked the receptionist if there was a doctor available. Ironically, the name of my new doctor sounds like "Dr. Surrendering." God has a sense of humor. While making the appointment I assured the good Lord, "I'm surrendering. I'm surrendering!"

So many times throughout our lives we are asked to surrender. That's so we can get good at it, because surrendering to God is important to our evolving apostolate. Oftentimes we are asked to surrender to circumstances way beyond our understanding. Sometimes answers present themselves and sometimes they do not. That is why we have faith. One of the many ways we can express our love for God is to trust in Him when we are vulnerable. Part of God's plan for my life has included enduring various health maladies for most of the past three years. What trials! I did have the privilege of meeting many wonderful doctors and their staff members. That previous spring I had a talk with God and informed Him I was willing to do all that He asked of me, but said that I needed to be well to do them properly. One Sunday I surprised myself by saying out loud in church, "**God, please fix me!**"

Trust. Surrender. Give thanks through everything. Pray. Hope. Plan. Keep going.

In the spring my doctor found a small lump during a routine exam and recommended further tests. Not long after that I found myself in a medical complex for the afternoon, waiting among other women wearing paper vests for our turn with the various diagnostic machines. I had the opportunity to meet more nice people. After a mammogram I was transferred to another waiting room where more women waited. It seemed wrong that we did not have access to chocolate. Had I known, I would have brought some along, for all of us! While waiting I reflected on all my sisters and brothers that would have their tests and not receive good news. I wondered who among us in the room would face such hardship.

In time I was brought to the dimly lit ultrasound room, and after a long while those tests were complete. Then I was told to await my meeting with the radiologist, another new doctor. The ultrasound technician led the radiologist into the room and I propped myself up. Something seemed amiss. The doctor introduced himself and proceeded to tell me how long he had been a radiologist and how many mammograms he had read. I listened intently as he listed his credentials, wondering where he was going with the impressive information. Then he proceeded to tell me that he had never seen a mammogram like mine in his entire career. He invited me into his viewing room to see my results. Before leaving the room I wanted one question answered right away. Was I healthy or not? He said I was.

In the viewing room the doctor lit the images up and I saw what looked like pictures of millions of stars up in the sky. I was fine, but the images were very unusual. The doctor recommended that I have an MRI, but I told him I had bigger medical fish to fry in my quest to feel well. I was stunned when he replied, **"God is trying to fix you!"** I said nothing to him about my prayer in church, but would have another opportunity to tell him in the very near future.

Now back to the story about my late-summer ear infection. Early that same year, the ring finger on my dominant hand started hurting. The finger looked fine but the pain got progressively worse, and after five months a sore developed that would not heal. Dr. Surrendering sent me to the hospital for an ultrasound of my finger. I had a hard time convincing the scheduler to give me an appointment because she had never heard of such a thing. I swore it was true.

At the hospital, a very nice person completed an ultrasound of my finger in another dimly lit room. Then, in walked the very same radiologist who read my unusual mammogram. The medical continuity was comforting. He did not remember me but he remembered my unusual mammogram. The doctor could not determine the problem with my finger. However, I took the opportunity to share with him the story of asking God to fix me and hearing him say at our last meeting "God is trying to fix you!" He in turn shared a story with me. Every day he says a rosary on his way to work. One day while driving to work disaster on the road was averted and he attributed the saved lives to the power of prayer. I have come to call such encounters "God moments" and they happen often.

I had to return to Dr. Surrendering. He took a picture of my finger as I wondered if it was my destiny to fill medical texts with my weird health issues. The good doctor prescribed a third round of antibiotics for the finger and the persistent ear problem, which had progressed to constant, throbbing pain on the left side of my head and pain radiating across my face to my nose and down to my throat.

As I continued with the new antibiotics I kept an eye on the sore finger. I began imagining what it would be like if I was no longer able to use that finger. How long would it take me to adjust to typing with nine fingers? I resolved that no matter what, I would keep on writing, with or without the finger. Whatever God wants.

One day it came to me that my finger was going to heal and then I was going to write a book. Well, the third dose of medication did the trick, my head stopped hurting, and my finger finally healed! For three weeks after that, I had a feeling something was going to happen. Something did happen: God told me to compile this book. After that, my boys collided in the driveway and Nick ended up in a cast. I met even more doctors, but that's another story.

So I started the new book and developed another health issue. I had a lump that was growing quickly and causing me increasing discomfort and pain. The morning of my appointment I had to take my son to the doctor. He had the flu. Then I went to my appointment in yet another new building. I felt at peace with my circumstances, knowing that God has a lot of work lined up for me to do yet. In small measure and in weird ways, I was called to assist God in His plan of salvation by carrying the cross of illness.

My newest specialist was absolutely lovely, very compassionate, and knowledgeable. She quickly determined that I had a cyst located by converging nerve endings that had filled with fluid. Her plan was to insert a needle guided by ultrasound into the cyst and draw out the fluid. She called a woman in to assist. I welcomed her as "an angel" and she informed me that she was no angel. I responded that for the purposes of this procedure she needed to be my angel. We all smiled as she consented. I really did not want to watch the process on the ultrasound screen, but they made me (ha ha). I told them to ignore all my painful facial expressions and assured them I was fine—just freaked out. One-two-three; we were done and I was looking at the fluid that was no longer my problem.

We delight God when we trust Him through all circumstances, for in doing so we live in imitation of His Son. If you are suffering from health problems, place yourself in God's hands completely. Allow Him to love you and care for you through other people. Trust. Surrender. Give thanks through everything. Hope. Plan. Keep going. Know that God is at work in you in a very special way.

—MICHELE ELENA BONDI

Chapter Five

Suffering

GOD, THE MONEY, AND THE SURPRISE ENDING

He is loving and generous and knows what we need.

Several years ago my daily morning routine consisted of dropping my children off at their schools, attending daily Mass, and then going to the same local restaurant in town where I worked on my first book. Over time I got to know the wonderful people who worked there and who took very good care of me while I worked. One day a waitress told me that a co-worker was diagnosed with cancer, required an operation, and the restaurant was planning on having a fundraiser for her. No date was set for the event so every once in a while I asked if a date had been selected.

One day I felt very strongly compelled not to wait until the fundraiser but to *give $100 to the woman without delay*. God must have been making progress with me, because that time I did not question His plans. I went to the bank, withdrew the money, and tucked the money in a bank envelope and put it in my purse. I had the money but no plan how to get it to the woman anonymously. I certainly did not want to be treated any differently at the restaurant nor did I want anyone to feel indebted to me. The money came from God and was given by God.

The next time I was at the restaurant I typed away, wondering how the transfer was to play out and fully planning to leave there without the money. A lovely waitress with whom I had spoken many times before came over to say hello. This time during our conversation she told me about a man she was taking for medical treatment once a week whom she had met while waiting to see her doctor. He had gone in for treatment on the wrong day and was told to return the next day. He responded that he had no way to get to the doctor the next day. The lovely woman, who did not even know the man, offered to pick him up and take him to his appointment the next day and has been taking him to his appointment every week since then. At that moment I knew that she was the one who was to take the money to the woman who was ill. I did not get another opportunity to speak to her again that day, so the money remained with me in my purse.

That weekend, my very kind neighbors visited us and asked us if we would like to have a bicycle. They had bought the bicycle for their grandsons to ride during visits and the boys had outgrown the bike. It was a darling bike in great shape and could be used by boys or girls. My daughter had outgrown her bicycle and was in need of a new one. Through that bicycle, *God gave us back the money in the envelope before it had even left my purse.*

The next time I saw my friend at the restaurant I told her about the money and she agreed to be the messenger. She understood that all the credit belonged to God and agreed to give the money anonymously to the woman who was ill. Not many days after that, the wonderful messenger approached me while I was writing and told me that she had found just the right card, put the $100 in the card, and then added money of her own! She reported that when the woman in need received the card and the money she was deeply touched and cried with joy.

After a while I stopped working at that restaurant. I found a different place closer to home with delicious hazelnut coffee and have been writing there ever since. About a year later I returned to the former restaurant and many of the kind waitresses whom I had gotten to know stopped by to say hello, including the one who had been ill. I asked her how she was feeling and she told me with a smile that she was doing well and was taking good care of her health by exercising, thanks to a kind person who had given her money with which she used to purchase—*a bicycle.*

God is so loving and generous and knows what we need! He is at work, in each one of us.

—MICHELE ELENA BONDI

How Jesus Made His Way to His Beloved in Isolation

Living in imitation of the One who loved us first.

In late fall I called my sister to wish her a happy birthday and she informed me that just the day before, she found out that she has stage III cancer. The world as we knew it changed forever. In the short time since being diagnosed, she has been through a week-long battery of tests, meetings with her oncology team, and doctor visits. She has endured a very difficult mental and physical trial. Shortly after she began treatment she developed a life-threatening infection and was admitted to the isolation unit of the hospital. After dropping my children off at school I went to daily Mass. Toward the end of Mass the idea came to me to bring the Eucharist to my sister. So after Mass I signed out a pyx and placed the Eucharist inside.

During the journey to pick up my mother before going on to the hospital I contemplated the fact that I was holding the Creator of the Universe in my hand! I also knew for sure that something amazing was going to happen. Something amazing was already happening!

Before entering my sister's hospital room in isolation, my mother and I donned masks to protect her from infection. I held the pyx out to my sister as we entered and greeted one another, and proudly proclaimed, "Guess Who I brought with me? I brought Jesus." My sister started to cry, and I was so moved by the tiny yet enormous presence of God there in the isolation unit of the huge medical complex. As I hugged my sister I cried too, and told her, "We suffer with you, because we love you."

My sister then said that she had called the chaplain that morning and asked him to please bring her Holy Communion. He would not because he had been exposed to many hospitalized people that morning and did not want to put her at any risk. I happily proclaimed to her that Jesus was going to make it to her, one way or another! He knew the desire of her heart and made sure He was there for her in her time of suffering.

After spending the afternoon with my sister, I took my mother home and she brought a letter in from her mailbox. It was from her sister in Germany and on the envelope there were four stamps, each one with a red rose on it! My sister loves roses, and this was a sign from our beloved St. Therese that she is with us, too.

Yesterday after Bible study a wonderful woman approached me after hearing the story and presented me with a pyx she had obtained in Rome. It has a picture of Pope John Paul II on it and is to be used as long as necessary to bring the Eucharist to my sister. He loves each one of us and wants to come to every one of us, no matter where we are.

—Anonymous

"KEEP YOUR FOCUS ON ETERNITY"

God's love for each of us is very personal.

One evening almost 10 years ago, I was resting in the spare bedroom of our former home and suddenly a huge book appeared before me. The book was open to a section that described the Sacrament of Marriage as designed by God for humanity. Words were visible on the two pages before me as in any book, but I understood what was written without having to read the words, and was deeply moved by the intelligence and great beauty of what was written. Then I was instructed to keep my focus on eternity.

God loves each one of us immensely. His love for you and me is deeply personal. Oh, that we would spend our lives adoring Him with a love that is deeply personal in return! How great is His mercy, His compassion! How caught up we get in things that are of no value to our souls and have no value for the souls of our brothers and sisters. We are to keep focused on that which is eternal.

At the time I saw the book, received information on the Sacrament of Marriage, and was instructed to focus on eternity, my marriage was ending. I did not even know it, but God knew. The Sacrament of Marriage is vital to God's plan for humanity. Pray that the Author of Marriage be invited to every wedding! Pray that all those called to the vocation of Holy Matrimony realize the value of their vow and go to God often for the strength and love needed to honor that promise.

I still reflect back on the moment when God offered me crucial information in advance of my divorce. He consoled me and guided me into the next phase of my evolving apostolate with His instruction to keep my focus on that which is eternal. Circumstances change throughout our lifetimes, and God's love transcends every one of them. Be comforted with the knowledge that eternal joy in the presence of God awaits the just in heaven.

Each one of us has been given a role to play in God's plan of salvation. Each one of us encounters suffering and loss on our way to eternity. God is always present to love us, guide us, teach us, strengthen us, and help us through every circumstance. God values us so much that He willed us into being so that we could spend eternity in His most loving presence.

About nine years after seeing the book, I walked into the chapel of a church in a neighboring city to visit with Jesus present in the Eucharist. I gasped out loud and had to look away after seeing a life-sized statue of Jesus scourged. If you ever doubt how much God loves you, meditate on the image of our beloved Jesus during His Passion and remember that He agreed to accept that which was ours to endure. Jesus loves us that much! Do not allow yourself to be tempted to think otherwise, and keep your focus on sharing that love with Him now and forever. Through every circumstance, in all that you do, keep your focus on eternity. We shall reap what we sow.

—MICHELE ELENA BONDI

I Am His Own

I heard a voice say, "Go to church."

I am an ordinary woman; there is nothing special about me. I grew up in a family where Mom was a devout Catholic and Dad was not. To this day I do not know if my father was baptized or raised in any faith. There is no one to ask.

I will not bore you with details about my life, as they are insignificant. I was a "Sunday" Catholic. God was Sunday. I went to Mass every Sunday, the first one of the morning so as not to wreck whatever plans my father had that day. Going to Mass guaranteed that I would not burn in Hell. What a chore it was to get up at the crack of dawn (or so I thought), to listen to a priest talk, get the Host, say a prayer and go home.

I remained a "Sunday" Catholic as a young adult. God was for Sunday. Little did I know that God was always with me. I followed my mother's path and married a non-Catholic man. Upon hearing his proposal of marriage, I quickly spoke up. "Only if our kids are raised as Catholics." I thought of them and their future with God first. So our children were raised as Catholics. Years have passed and we are very proud of the wonderful people they have become.

About 11 years ago we found ourselves living in a small town in Illinois after my husband's promotion. It was very difficult to make friends there. Being an outgoing person, I was miserable. I could feel myself falling into a deep depression. My kids and husband made the transition with varying degrees. My husband was thrilled with his job and the kids finally adjusted to their new environment. For them, all was right with the world.

One morning when the kids and my husband were off to school and work, I woke up to face another day alone. As I lay there I started to cry, and being depressed and angry, said out loud, "Why should I even get up, I have nothing to get up for!"

I heard a voice say "Go to church." The voice sounded as if it were in my bedroom. I was terrified. I was struck with awe that I would receive an answer! I suddenly realized that the only person that I did not turn to was God! I got up, went to church, found out the Mass schedule, and turned not only my problems but my joys over to God.

He listens and is patient and I feel special. I know that there is nothing that I can't share with Him. I attend Mass almost every day. I especially enjoy being in the chapel before Mass—having Our Lord all to myself for a little bit. I now realize that God is with us always and is not just for Sunday. I am an ordinary woman, but I am special in God's eyes. I am His own.

—LYNN CZAR

How an Accident with a Dog Brought Me Closer to Christ

A summer encounter with a dog and a rope.

One sunny day my children and I were having fun with friends in our backyard. Our friends brought along their newest family member, a very playful medium-sized dog. Her collar was attached to a long rope, which was anchored in the ground in the middle of the yard. She happily ran around with the children as we all enjoyed a glorious day.

The accident happened very quickly, and although I saw it coming just before it happened there was no time for me to react. I do remember my friend gasping at the sight of what was about to happen to me. The dog was running along with the children in the yard and the rope attached to her collar formed a big loop on the grass. My right foot happened to be inside of that circle and as she ran the rope rapidly made a tighter circle until it completely surrounded my ankle. The dog came to a sudden stop as the rope completed its circle and cut into my flesh. The pain was excruciating. After my friend secured her dog I was able to remove the rope from inside of and around my leg. Pain and more pain. Everyone felt very bad that I had been hurt. However, the accident proved to be a tremendous blessing.

113

As we all studied the gash in my leg, I thought of the lashes and the gashes in the precious flesh of our beloved Jesus during His scourging. There was one very painful, accidental gash in my leg—but our Savior had so many. His suffering was no accident; it was purposeful. He chose to pay the debt we owed. He loves us THAT much.

Then Pilate took Jesus and had him flogged. And the soldiers wove a crown of thorns and put it on his head, and they dressed him in a purple robe. They kept coming up to him, saying, "Hail, King of the Jews!" and striking him on the face. John 19: 1-3.

The pain in my leg remained for days and I was reminded of the gash often, especially every morning in the shower. When water hit it the pain was terrible. Although the injury caused me pain, I felt great love at the same time because the pain reminded me of Jesus' great love for me. Like Jesus' pain, my pain was accomplishing something good. My children learned from the experience and now when they get a cut they think about what Jesus endured for their salvation. By being grateful for the good that my suffering accomplished, I understood more personally that a Savior who accepted such unfathomable suffering to redeem every single one of us is one very loving Savior indeed.

"O Jesus, many times in my life I have preferred Barabbas to you. There is no way that I can undo those choices but to make my way to your feet and beg your forgiveness. But that is so humiliating, for you wear the garment of a fool, and you bear in your hand the reed scepter of a mock king! It is so hard for me to do penance and to admit that I am guilty! It is so hard to be seen with you, who are wearing your crown of thorns. It is hard! But let me see, Jesus, that it is harder to wear the crown of thorns"[9]

A three-inch scar remains on my leg, while Jesus' love remains in my life. Most loving Jesus, I accept Your offer of salvation and sanctification. May my life be a living testimony of my gratitude to You for suffering in my place. My sweet Jesus, I love you back!

—MICHELE ELENA BONDI

---

9 Fulton J. Sheen, The Way of the Cross (Our Sunday Visitor, Inc.: Indiana) p. 8-9.

Learning, Loving, Leaning, and Letting Go

You have a team, and God is on it.

One late summer day I spent several hours at the Cardiovascular Center at the University of Michigan Medical Center in Ann Arbor, Michigan. I accompanied one of my dearest friends there for a consultation regarding open-heart surgery. While our children played together in the waiting room, she spoke to her heart surgeon and I listened and took notes. What a truly wonderful person the surgeon turned out to be. What an amazing apostolate he has!

The surgeon began by showing us a model of the heart and explained in detail how the heart works. As he spoke, I was astounded in a way I never had been before at how complex and amazing our systems are. Perhaps that was because this lesson was personal. I had a quick moment with God right then and there. I told Him that this model and the accompanying explanation were enough proof for me that He exists. What an amazing human engineer God is!

That day was incredibly amazing and also very difficult. It was a day of travel, a day of waiting, a day of discovery, a day of shared sorrow, a day of service, a day when many disciplineships came together for the sake of my friend, whom God loves very much.

As my friend and I spoke on the long journey home, with me driving and getting us lost and she finding our way, we discussed her situation, what the doctor said, what we learned, and what was to come next. We acknowledged her great suffering and her concern. We discussed what she would say to her son and how he was handling the situation. We determined that together with many other people, we are a team. God is on her team, and cares for her through us while providing her with the strength she needs to persevere.

God's ways are mysterious indeed, and in my friend's case things have yet to play out. We discussed the doctor's sage comments to continue living life filled with joy and not fear. We also discussed how sometimes we have to let God direct our lives, let go of what we have no control over, and accept what He has in the works for us in any given situation.

How our lives are so interconnected, how much each of our missions benefit countless others, how many opportunities we have to love and serve each other throughout our lifetimes. God is there, on everyone's team, working all things out for our greater good while providing us with strength to persevere and evidence that He is always with us.

—MICHELE ELENA BONDI

God Hears You!

Pray with confidence and reverence His judgment.

"Our prayer is an incense which God receives with extreme pleasure."[10]
—St. John Vianney, from *Catechism on Prayer*

A few weeks ago I got a call during a meeting to pick up my ill seventh-grade son from school. This year he has had the flu, a virus, and a head cold. The rest of us have contracted various illnesses too, but Nick has suffered the most. Currently he has allergies and headaches. It seems we have not had a week go by this year where everyone in our family was healthy. The constant illnesses have been a source of great frustration for me.

Meetings have had to be postponed, schools called, sick children tended to, homework acquired and completed, my work delayed. For the past three months much less was accomplished than I had hoped. My frustration grew with each passing week as someone came down with something else. Many significant events were occurring simultaneously. Day after day, I wondered why God was having so many things happen to us at the same time. In addition, my cell phone got crushed in a door, my flash drive ended up in the washer, my laptop stopped working, my daughter and I were

117

involved in a hit-and-run accident before school, my e-mail was hacked, my credit card had to be stopped due to fraud, someone left a dead skunk in a plastic bag on our driveway, and my son and I were almost hit by a truck. My frustration mounted and the collective burden seemed more than I could carry.

Just when I had myself convinced that no one could possibly get sick again, at least for a little while, I got that call from Nick's school. At that moment I resolved to stop wrestling with God. My resistance was not changing anything and was causing me to become even more frustrated. I left my meeting to get Nick and did so with a new spirit of resignation and reverence for whatever the good Lord had in mind. As we drove home, Nick and I had a discussion about cooperating with God's will. Then my son told me something that totally surprised me.

Nick said that he had been suffering so much because he had asked God to allow him to take on the suffering of someone else. Can you just imagine what ran through my mind at that moment? I was so impressed with his spiritual depth and the great courage it took him to ask God to grant such a noble request. That is Catholic courage! How often we ask God for things that would make our lives easier or more comfortable, things that benefit us and not particularly other people, things that do not coincide with God's much better plans for us.

Holy Week is an opportune time to consider Jesus' example. He accepted the will of our Father and redeemed each of us at the cost of His own life. How often our human nature defies the will of God and asks instead for what we want, sometimes at the cost of other people. True love is sacrificial, true love serves, true love seeks what is in the best interest of others, true love seeks to accomplish the will of God. Nick had asked God to allow him to suffer for others. After contemplating for a moment what Nick's prayer had cost us all the past few months, I turned to him and said in jest, "Don't do that!" In the spirit of joy that can be found in divine resignation, we shared a hearty laugh. What a fine young man my Nick is.

How easy it is to pray when we want or need something. Prayer that yields great fruit is prayer that gives glory to God, thanks Him, and rejoices to be in His presence. Life-changing prayer asks that His will be accomplished in us, and asks that we be allowed to shoulder the burden of another. Only twice in my entire life have I had the courage to ask God to allow me to suffer in someone else's place. Once I asked the good Lord to allow me to take on the sorrow of a friend who was grieving to alleviate her suffering. God answered my prayer and I cried for a week.

Perhaps our prayers would be different if we were conscious of what prayers God always answers. In the thought-provoking book *Prayers God Always Answers* by Anthony DeStefano, DeStefano points out that God answers us when we ask Him to show that He exists, when we ask Him to forgive us, work through us, and help us persevere. He responds to our requests for peace, courage, and wisdom, when we ask Him to bring good out of bad situations, and when we ask Him to help us discern. I add that He allows us to participate with Him in the salvation of souls. Can you think of any other prayers that God always answers?

"God has created my heart only for Himself. He asks me to give it to Him that He may make it happy."[11] —St. John Vianney, *Eucharistic Meditation.*

Once a woman asked Mother Angelica about praying for a certain intention. She responded, "I would pray. If you talk to Jesus about it, He hears you. He doesn't mind being reminded, once a day. I wouldn't gripe and nag. He hears you. He knows."

St. Pio said, "Hope, pray, and don't worry." Venerable Father Solanus Casey said we should thank God ahead of time.

Pray, and in your prayers praise God and tell Him you love Him. Thank Him for His many blessings, including the ones you are not aware of. Talk to Him from your heart. Ask Him for that which will be for your eternal benefit. Allow Him to work through you in the way He best sees fit. Renew your trust in Him and reverence His judgments. Remember others in your prayers. God loves you. God hears you!

"Ask our Lord for the grace to think only of Him and to desire only to please Him in all you do during your whole life."[12] —St. John Vianney, from *Sermon on the First Commandment*

—MICHELE ELENA BONDI

---

10 Compiled and Arranged by W.M.B., *Thoughts of The Cure'D'Ars* (Rockford, IL: Tan Books and Publishers, Inc., 1967), p. 63.

11 Compiled and Arranged by W.M.B., *Thoughts of The Cure'D'Ars* (Rockford, IL: Tan Books and Publishers, Inc., 1967), p. 22.

12 Compiled and Arranged by W.M.B., *Thoughts of The Cure'D'Ars* (Rockford, IL: Tan Books and Publishers, Inc., 1967), p. 63.

Saying Goodbye to an American Hero

Heaven gained another from "The Greatest Generation."

In late 2009 I attended the burial service for my Uncle Jeff, a veteran of World War II and an American hero. He was not my uncle by blood but was an uncle by love, not only to me but to many others.

Jeff was married to Mary for over 60 years. She preceded him in death by a year and a half, and in His time the Good Lord honored Jeff's request to be reunited with her in eternity. Jeff and Mary had hoped to become parents but lost multiple children before birth. So they adopted rescued dogs and loved other people's children instead.

When I was a child, my father met Mary at church after Dad joined the parish council. Dad and Mom and Jeff and Mary shared a mutual love for the Lord and became fast friends. Uncle Jeff and Aunt Mary lived on a canal four large blocks from us and we spent many hours visiting at each other's homes. Aunt Mary enrolled me in the Blue Army and always took me out for pizza on my birthday. She made brown scapulars and was always busy with church work and defending the unborn.

When my father was critically ill at the age of 39, Jeff and Mary were there to help our young family and see us through. She and I shared a friend, St. Therese of Lisieux, and the day I was confirmed the three of us stood together with Aunt Mary as my sponsor. When Dad died at the age of 46, Jeff and Mary continued to look after our family. Uncle Jeff stood in my late Father's place to walk me down the aisle the day I married. During visits he reminisced about the war, and enjoyed sharing stories about growing up in his large family. He honored us by passing on the family nickname "Butch" to my oldest son. He nicknamed my middle child "Rusty" and my daughter "Goldie." Uncle Jeff had a piece of the Berlin Wall, which he gave me. Not only was that gift very symbolic, it was also a sign of things to come in my future. I will always treasure that symbol of freedom, which is every person's right as predestined by God.

Uncle Jeff was an American soldier and had the courage to drive the ammo truck. He fought in the Battle of the Bulge, the last major Nazi offensive against the Allies in World War II. He liberated a concentration camp and let me hold the metal cross that a man had made while a prisoner in the camp. That cross was a reminder that love, faith, and hope remain—even in the worst of situations. Uncle Jeff was the first American soldier that many saw the day the camp was liberated. Six months after the war ended, Uncle Jeff was returning to the United States when his ship ran into a typhoon, was blown far off course, and had to be rescued.

With Uncle Jeff's extended family scattered across the country and being survived by only one sister, the number of people at his funeral service was small. Two people offered their memories. A nephew told the story of how Uncle Jeff went to the East Coast to get him after both his parents had died. Aunt Mary and Uncle Jeff took him in and he lived with them until he went into the military. Then they invited him back after he got out of the service. A man greatly beloved by Jeff and Mary sat in front of me. During his youth he was taken in and nurtured by Jeff and Mary until he was ready to venture out on his own. What a difference their love made in the lives of these men!

I did not stand up and I did not offer a speech to the small group of people who were there to share their love for Jeff, to witness the difference he made in their lives, and to see him off into eternity. But here is what I might have said:

"I have known Uncle Jeff since I was a child. Through the years people would ask me if he was my mom's brother or my dad's brother, but he was neither. He was everyone's brother. Jeff defended his country in World War II, worked hard all his life, and looked after his family well. His family included anyone who was in need. At times that was me, and I thank you, Uncle Jeff, for what you did for our world at large and for me as an individual. You truly lived in imitation of Christ.

"My heart is filled with joy knowing that you and Aunt Mary are together once again, finally enjoying the company of the many children you lost so early in this life. Your family ended up being one of the largest of all! I love you forever, and look forward to living down the street from you and Aunt Mary in Heaven, on the canal."

—MICHELE ELENA BONDI

CHAPTER SIX

MIRACLES

Miracle or Coincidence?

"Atheists don't believe in miracles; the faithful don't need them to believe." —Unknown

I was born into an Albanian Muslim family 86 years ago. My father had earned a Ph.D. in history and philosophy in Vienna (Austria). My mother had attended a Catholic middle school run by nuns. For political reasons, my father and the rest of the family escaped from Albania and eventually reached Austria. I started school and on the first day of school, all of us, teachers and pupils, went to church. There, at the church of the Sacred Heart of Jesus during Mass, I distinctly heard God calling me to be a Catholic. That voice would resonate within me for my entire life.

A few years later we moved to Italy. I was attending the 11th grade and was also a member of the city choir. At one point, in 1941, the choir traveled to Rome for a contest. One Sunday, of 3600 members from all over the country (half of them boys and the other half girls), about 300 boys went to Mass while the rest went sightseeing. We wore uniforms similar to those of the military. Before Mass at St. Peter's Basilica, a priest walked by our group. A clown (you can never have a group of 300 youngsters without a clown) approached the priest and asked whether we could see the Holy Father. The priest looked somewhat taken aback while the rest of us would have gladly strangled our 'clown.' Believe it or not, at the end of Mass the same priest approached us and informed us that the Holy Father was expecting us. Well, we marched across St. Peter's Square, entered one of the wings . . . and stood there gaping at the mural paintings by Michelangelo, paintings we were just studying about in our history of art classes. The one that stands out in my mind was the painting where God touches Adam's hand and Adam, the first man, comes to life.

We climbed some stairs and found ourselves in a splendid garden. From there they escorted us into the small reception hall and 300 of us filled about one third of the room. The large reception hall was for 2000 couples! The Holy Father, Pius XII, approached and spoke to each and every one of us.

He asked me when we were leaving. "This coming Tuesday, Holy Father," I replied.

He moved to the boy next to me, the first of the tenors, and asked him: "How old are you, my son?"

"Fifteen, Holy Father."

The Pope shook his head, "Too young, too young." Obviously, we were not too young to sing in a choir. It dawned on me later that the priest had thought we were soldiers because of our uniforms, and the Holy Father had agreed to see us as we had attended Mass and wanted to see the Holy Father. He had therefore accepted to make time for us as we were probably going to war.

Coincidence born of confusion? Probably. The Holy Father gave us medals he had blessed and I proudly wore mine—until I got home.

"What's the meaning of that medal?" Dad asked me. Having heard my explanation, he ordered me to take it off, and I did. Dad believed in God, the Creator of the universe. He did not believe in any religion that he considered man's creation based on hierarchy, power, economic interests, politics, and discipline.

The story of the medal, however, does not stop here. I attended medical school in Padua, the city of St. Anthony, in 1941. Later I planned on escaping to Austria. I had gone to a pawn shop and wanted to buy gold as Yugoslav currency was of little value abroad. Buying gold could make the owner suspicious. I claimed that I wanted to get married but the two wedding bands he brought out were too cheap for what I had in mind. When I asked for something more expensive, he brought a chain with a medal. The price was right, but I feared that he might alert the police. I paid, got out in a hurry, and when I felt safe, stopped to see what I had bought. What I was looking at was a beautiful, 18-carat gold chain with the medal of St. Anthony. A wave of deep religious feelings flooded my heart and mind. How many times had I gone to the Basilica of St. Anthony while in Padua?

During the years that followed, I was never truly hard pressed and never had the need to sell the medal and chain of St. Anthony. I still wear it after so many years.

Years after I was released from a communist prison, I wanted to visit Dad, who had been transferred to a far-away jail. This happened around 1951. A friend gave me a forged travel order that would allow me to travel by bus and sleep in the local hotel. During my return trip the conductor on the bus put me up front and two other civilians, who were traveling together, in the back. It turned out that the two were members of the dreaded secret police traveling in civilian clothes. They objected that they were put in the back. One word led to another, they insulted the conductor, and had me get off the bus to see whether I had a forged travel pass. They had me empty my pockets and went through my bundle of papers, one by one. I could anticipate what was going to happen to me: torture, pain, and prison. What was worse was that my friend, who had forged the pass, had a wife and two little children. And I was the one responsible for their upcoming persecution and sufferings.

Having been unsuccessful in their search, the two officers returned the bundle to me. I was allowed to get on the bus and continue my trip. It turned out that they had arrested the conductor and had tortured him for several days as punishment for his 'insolent language.' Two years later, I escaped from Albania and wound up in Greece. When the CIA examined the same bundle of papers, they found and commented on the forged pass. It must have been with the bundle all that time.

In 1952 I took to the mountains to escape from Albania to Yugoslavia. It took me three months (fall and winter) to finally cross the mountains and rivers. One night we had to walk on a tree trunk to cross a raging torrent. The water was above the trunk almost as much as underneath it. Everybody crossed. I was the last in line. As I stepped on the tree trunk, I could see myself slipping and breaking a leg, if not worse. My companions would have had to continue marching toward the border. I would have been left behind and this would be the death of me. I froze, unable to move either foot. My friends were motioning to me; they were in a hurry. I prayed to the Blessed Mother, from the bottom of my heart. When I opened my eyes, I was on the other side of the torrent. I don't remember having made even one step, but there I was! Coincidence?

While escaping, circumstances forced us to spend three weeks in a cave. Our hiding place was barely enough for my three companions and me. I, the tallest, was squeezed in at the entrance to the cave where the opening was at its narrowest. We suffered physical discomforts and a starvation diet. One day, I approached the edge of the cliff near the cave. My feet slipped. I fell but was fortunate enough to grab a small root sticking out of the mountainside. It did not break. I was able to reach the bottom of a bush overhead and I pulled myself up. I turned around and looked at the gorge with the river several hundred feet below. Once more, my time had not come. Some may say this, too, was coincidence.

After Albania was taken over by the communists in November 1944, Dad and I were arrested on the first day of the takeover. In prison, both of us were put in isolation with a handful of other prisoners, among them a former prior of the Franciscans.

One day, Dad was standing next to the Franciscan who was sitting on his cot. "How is it possible that one drop of the blood of Christ can wash away the sins of the world?" he asked the Franciscan. I remember the question vividly as it burned itself into my mind. I do not recall, however, the Franciscan's answer. It had to be based on faith rather than human logic. The years went by and one day at the moment I was receiving Holy Communion, above the head of the priest, I saw the scene I had witnessed in prison many years ago: Dad bending over the Franciscan as he had asked his question. But this time, Dad turned toward me, smiled, and said in English: "Now I understand."

I have listed a few events that, in retrospect, are out of the ordinary. I am sure any adult could look back and come up with comparable incidents. Are they miracles or just coincidence? I think it is up to each man or woman to draw what conclusions make more sense according to personal experience and circumstances. I know where I stand. If I eat a good meal, I know that somewhere there is a cook that prepared it. How could I look at the universe and its incredible complexity, at the beauty, the details, and fragrances that surround us in nature, at the depth and breadth and mystery of life surrounding us? Why would 'coincidence' offer a better explanation than 'faith'?

I have witnessed and marveled at human love, goodness, and self-sacrifice. Let others explain away motherly love, readiness to share even in extreme poverty, willingness to die for one another. For me, such virtue comes only from a source beyond human limitations. Praised be His goodness, His willingness to forgive, and His readiness to die for us, so that one day we too may be able to say, "Now we understand."

—GENE X. KORTSHA

THE SCAPULAR STORY

How God interceded for a brother to us all.

Several years ago my family and I visited the tomb of Venerable Fr. Solanus Casey at St. Bonaventure in Detroit. During our initial visit there, my sister suggested that we touch our scapulars to Fr. Solanus' tomb and so we did. We felt called to go back, and returned two weeks later. While browsing in the gift shop I suddenly felt instructed to purchase a "woman's" scapular. I continued to look around and was unable to think of anyone I knew who needed one, so I did not purchase the scapular. Once again, I looked to my own limited knowledge instead of trusting in God, who knows everything!

A few weeks later on my way home after Sunday Mass, I was at the scene of a terrible accident. A young man on a motorcycle was struck by a sport utility vehicle on a five-lane, 50-miles-per-hour stretch of well-traveled road. The force of the impact hurled the man horizontally across four lanes of the road and he landed in front of the car ahead of me. Traffic stopped abruptly. The fact that the man was not hit again by another vehicle was in itself a miracle. I was very afraid to see the condition of the man who was most certainly injured, so I decided to remain in my van. Competing with that decision was a strong prompting that I was to leave my vehicle and go to him.

I resisted, certain that there was nothing I could do to help the injured man. I remained in my vehicle, again relying on my own knowledge instead of trusting in God. However, God had something very important for me to give him! Once again, I felt strongly compelled to get out of my van and go to the man. God's will was very clear and He provided me with the courage I needed to leave my vehicle and approach the motorcyclist.

The scene was as horrifying as I had feared. The man's injuries were severe and his broken body convulsed violently on the road. Crowds of people stood frozen on the sides of the road, weeping. As I wept, I had an understanding of this man as a brother to us all. While approaching the man, *I understood that I was to remove my scapular and place it on him!* In that instant I knew that the woman's scapular I was instructed to buy while in the gift shop at St. Bonaventure was meant for me, to replace the one I was wearing.

Weeks before the accident, God had already planned that my scapular, touched to the tomb of Fr. Solanus, would be given to the injured man as his life hung in the balance. A firefighter on the scene placed the scapular on the man for me. I was filled with an overwhelming desire to pray to the Virgin Mary and knew that she was there interceding for him, as a most loving mother would. I was astounded to witness how the young man was given this pivotal intervention by God, along with Our Lady and Father Solanus. What love, what mercy!

Very few people approached the injured man. The first one on the scene was a man with a cell phone who called 911. The firemen had arrived after I did. There was another man who had also arrived just after I did. He was taller than me, had white hair, and was dressed like a priest. When I saw him, I could not believe how important it was for the injured man that a priest was on the scene. I said to the man, "Thank heaven you are here!" He spoke only to me and unlike everyone else on the scene, he was so serene and at peace. I do not remember what he said to me, just that he was not affected in the same way as the rest of us were. He never approached the injured man. Looking back, I believe that he was there for some reason for me. Just as quickly as he appeared he was gone. I believe that he left me with the same supernatural peace that he had and an absolute trust in the will of God.

I felt compelled to remain at the scene until the paramedics arrived and to instruct them that the scapular was to remain with the injured man. Once that was accomplished, I felt divine permission to leave. At that very moment a police officer approached me and showed me a way to depart the area.

On the way home, I knew for certain that God's most perfect will had been accomplished in all that had just taken place. A feeling of total consolation superseded any worry for the man despite his horrific condition. I experienced incredible peace and understood that we should trust in God always. The profound peace, consolation, and joy I felt remained with me for two months. The remarkable events of that day left me with absolutely no doubt that we must unite ourselves to God's divine will and trust Him, no matter how tragic events appear to our human perception. I also witnessed first-hand the powerful intercessors we have in the saints, and in Our Lady through the brown scapular.

—MICHELE ELENA BONDI

WAS IT TOO LATE TO PRAY?

"We don't need certainty. We need trust."

L ike many people, I have been praying, one way or another, for a long time. And, also like many people, maybe not always in the right way. For instance, a number of years ago, our oldest son was bitten behind the ear by a rabid badger while sleeping in a tent at a Boy Scout camp. I won't go into all the details. That's another story, as they say. But, briefly, he had to begin rabies shots—which should have been started immediately, but, due to circumstances, were begun late.

There was every indication that it might have been too late to prevent rabies from setting in. Naturally, we began to pray and asked everyone we knew to pray. But I had a problem with prayer. Somewhere, deep down, I had a hidden reservation that it was too late to pray. After all, if the natural process leading to rabies had already begun, would God "interfere" in that process? If the apple has already fallen from the table, should we pray for God to stop it before it hits the floor, since He is the author of the law of gravity? Wouldn't that be asking for a miracle?

Now, I never doubted that God can, and does, perform miracles. But, somehow I struggled with the idea that He would do that in this case. Wouldn't that be asking too much? So, caught in this dilemma, I decided to have a discussion with our pastor. What came out of that conversation gave me some insights on prayer that have stayed with me for a long time. The only one I will mention here is that we sometimes want to limit God in the way we ourselves are limited. But, for one thing, God is essentially outside of time and space. He can affect the outcome of events even before they happen.

He knows that we are going to pray for something long before we actually pray for it, even long before we even exist. Assuming God can only act according to our own limited experience really limits God. That is something we can't do and shouldn't try to do, especially in prayer. That insight has stayed with me for a long time and has helped many times in prayer. Mother Theresa once said (at the risk of misquoting her), "We don't need certainty. We need trust."

Oh, by the way, our son went through the rabies shots well and is living a happy and healthy life. Our prayers were answered.

—TED

TODAY I WITNESSED A MIRACLE!

And in a way, so did you.

Every time I receive the Precious Blood of Jesus in Holy Communion, I receive it in the name of all of humanity. I receive Him for all those who have died, all those who are living, and all those who are yet to be born. In a way, you and I received Jesus together today. We are all called to live in imitation of Christ, we are all called to love one another and do all we can to help one another. What better way to love each other than to offer our brothers and sisters a spiritual Communion!

I love the moment when, just before Communion, the priest holds up the chalice filled with the Blood of Jesus and above it holds in his other hand the small Host that each of us receives, in contrast with the larger Host that is held up during the consecration. What a beautiful, loving moment to be able to witness our unfathomable, immeasurable, uncontainable God become so tiny so that He can come to every single one of us. He loves us that much!

As I waited in line for my turn to receive Jesus this morning, I

looked up at the beautiful life-sized crucifix behind the altar and contemplated what Jesus endured for each one of us. We have our faults
and He loves us anyway. He beckons us and welcomes us to His table
to share in His love.

Today I witnessed a miracle and in a way, so did you! Thank you
Jesus for loving each one of us so much. May we never take Your love for
granted and do all we can to love You in return.

—MICHELE ELENA BONDI

The Phone Call and an Answer to Prayer

God loves every single one of us.

In July 2009, I called a Marriott in Utah to exchange points for a hotel room in Quebec City for the following month. The agent said that a room was available but he didn't know how to pronounce the name of the street, "Place d'Youville. I helped pronounce it and explained, "That street is named after Ste. Marguerite d'Youville, the foundress of the Grey Nuns."

He responded, "My wife is a devout Catholic but I don't know if I believe in God. Can I tell you my story?"

Of course I said "Yes." He told me that he grew up in the Mormon Church and was taught that people of color had the stain of Cain and were rejected by Christ. When he finished high school he joined the army, went to Georgia, and met beautiful African Americans that were so wonderful that it negated what he had been taught. He left the Mormon Church. He explained that since then he has seen how people make up what they think God is like so he now believes that there is probably no God. I responded, "Can I tell you a true story that I recently heard on Ave Maria radio?"

141

He said "Yes."

This is the story: A young man named Ed grew up in a Protestant denomination but when he started high school, his family stopped going to church and he became an agnostic. One day during his senior year, he was hitchhiking, and a man picked him up and said to him, "Jesus loves you."

Ed responded, "Don't talk to me like that!!" He became mean and vulgar and said, "Let me out." So the man pulled over and let Ed out.

The following week, Ed's sister asked him to go to a youth group meeting and there he saw the same man who had picked him when he was hitchhiking! He was the leader of the youth group and he once again said to Ed, "Jesus loves you."

Again Ed responded, "Don't say that to me." However, he continued going to the youth group.

Someone gave him the books *The Cross and the Switchblade* and *Run, Baby, Run,* which are accounts of a minister going to Harlem to evangelize the gangs and their conversion stories. Ed was just amazed at these stories and so on Good Friday he went to his former church, knelt down, and said "Jesus, if You are real, show me." He was filled with the love of the Lord, so much so that he thought his heart was going to burst.

Then Ed asked, "What about the Holy Spirit?" He saw a benign lightning in front of him that went through him and he began to pray and sing in tongues. He was absolutely astounded.

The next day was Holy Saturday and Ed went to the pastor and described his experience to him. The pastor responded, "That is biblical and charismatic but you don't belong in this church."

Ed wondered where he would go, began saying the "Our Father," and heard a voice say, "I will lead you home." That afternoon a Catholic friend from high school called and asked Ed to go to the Easter Vigil with him that night, and he agreed to go. When he got there they were reading many Scriptures; Ed had been taught that Catholics do not read the Bible. Now he thought they were going to read the whole Bible. Then the celebrant, a bishop, gave a homily about our relationship with Jesus and described what Ed had experienced the previous day!

After the homily he thought the people were leaving but realized that they were headed for the front. Ed heard a voice say, "This is my Body and my Blood you're receiving."

When he got to the front of the line, the bishop said, "The Body of Christ."

Not knowing how to respond, Ed answered, "Okay."

On the way back to his pew, he again heard the voice say, "I've brought you home."

At the time, Ed was going to the University of Minnesota and was studying to be a nuclear physicist. His parents told him not to let his new religion get in the way of his career. He joined the Newman Club, met a girl, and fell in love. They were both on fire for the faith and wanted to get married but he knew that her father, who was a judge, would never agree. In the meantime, Ed doubted his career choice and decided to go on a retreat to seek the Lord's will.

During the retreat he opened the Bible at Matthew and read, "Some people are born eunuchs and others are eunuchs for the Kingdom." He wondered, *What does that mean? Do You want me to check into the priesthood? I'll flip the Bible and where my finger lands, I'll know that is what You want.* His finger landed on Psalm 110: "You are a priest forever." He thought to himself, *That can't be, I'll try again.* He made sure he got past Psalm 110 and Matthew and landed in Hebrews, reading "You are a priest forever."

Next he had to tell his girlfriend. When he told her, she started laughing. Ed asked, "Why?"

She replied, "Two weeks ago, the Lord told me He wants me to be a nun."

He is now Fr. Ed Friede, pastor of Christ the King parish in Ann Arbor, Michigan. They have 23 seminarians at that parish.

After I finished telling the hotel agent the story, he said that he had goosebumps and concluded, "That is an amazing story."

I said to him, "All you need to do is ask the Lord to reveal Himself to you and He will."

He answered, "I don't know if I can do that."

Then I said, "You have a free will and you don't have to, but I want you to remember one thing. If you had been the only person in the world, Jesus would have died for you."

"Thank you," he said. "I will tell my wife."

I was totally moved by this experience. God can use us at any time if we just make ourselves available. I'm sure that man's wife has been praying for him for years. With God, all things are possible. So I'm praying for that man and asked him to contact me at any time.

I know this is a long story, but it's absolutely amazing. I heard it this spring on Al Kresta's and Peter Herbeck's radio shows and I've met Fr. Ed. He's an incredible and holy priest.

—Rejeanne Buckley

THE FALL LUNCHEON AND ALL THOSE LEAVES!

Do your best and let God handle the rest.

We have been blessed with 14 beautiful trees on our property. Spring is beautiful, summer is beautiful, fall is beautiful. I love to look up in the summer and contemplate that God knows how many leaves are on each tree. The fall color is just extraordinary in our neighborhood with its many mature trees.

By November, fallen leaves blanket the entire area. Last year my family made the decision to rake the leaves ourselves, compost them in our garden, and enjoy working together as a family. Oh, what a job! We had the determination, the rakes, the barrels, and the energy. What we lacked was time, and gathering up the leaves on our property with the tools we had was going to take us a long, long time. The sun was setting earlier and basketball practice had started.

When will we find the time to rake all those leaves? I wondered.

One warm and sunny Saturday was the ideal day to get a lot of leaf raking accomplished. As we pulled out of our driveway shortly after 11:00 a.m. my thoughts were on the leaves and responsibly gathering them up so they would not blow on the yards around us, for our neighbors work hard to keep their yards tidy. We were on our way to a benefit luncheon hosted by The Icon Dei Guild, the first benefit we would attend as a family. I factored the benefit into our budget by using the money we were saving by not hiring anyone to do the leaves.

When will we find the time to rake all those leaves? I asked God to handle it as we drove away.

The lovely luncheon was held at a beautiful hall. The event raised funds for Guest House, whose primary mission "is to provide the information, treatment and care needed to ensure that clergy, religious and seminarians suffering from alcoholism and other specified addictions have the very best opportunity for quality recovery. A related mission is to provide the servants of the Church education and other resources that will foster and enhance recovery." (www.guesthouse.org)

How blessed we were to attend this benefit, meet lovely new people, enjoy fellowship with friends from our parish who were also there, and enjoy a delicious meal, which included great coffee and dessert! We listened as the speaker gave a very passionate and motivating speech encouraging us to live our Catholic faith to the fullest and witness to others. How powerful!

My daughter was given a pumpkin pin by a kind lady and bought a beautiful rose pin. She even had the winning number for the snowman centerpiece on our table! So many blessings so freely given to us as we sought to help our priests who, as our speaker reminded us, are the ones that bring us Jesus.

After the benefit, we returned home and worked for an hour on the leaves. We moved a lot of leaves in that hour, but most of the yard was still blanketed. Then we left for St. Mary's of the Hills for Reconciliation. We were so happy to have received God's forgiveness and abundant graces as we prepared our souls for Andre receiving the Sacrament of Confirmation in a few weeks.

As we pulled out of the driveway I wondered anew: *When are we going to get to the rest of those leaves? God, I trust in you. Please handle it.*

Reconciliation was held in the lovely chapel of a beautiful church. While waiting for Reconciliation to begin, we encountered a couple who had just married. They were filled with such joy and spoke to us after ringing the church bells. We shared their joy with them and marveled at the beautiful wedding gift they had received on such a beautiful fall day! We prayed for them after they left. We saw two priests that we are blessed to know, we were forgiven for our sins, and then we ran into a friend on our way out. So much to be grateful for!!

When we returned home to the leaves, my middle guy was not doing too much leaf raking. Darkness was descending. Nick developed a fever. Now we were down a man. *When are we going to finish these leaves?* I wondered. We completed the side yard and went in for the night.

The next morning Nick's fever was higher and he was unable to help us with the leaves. "God, please make it all happen," I prayed. I had been feeling very much at peace. Then the doorbell rang.

A young man was at the door and out in the yard were many young people with rakes. *They were raking our leaves!* They had bagged up leaves in the yards of neighbors along the street to the left of our house and were raking leaves in several of my neighbors' yards. They would not take any money. In fact, the kids paid $3.00 each to participate. They were from Kensington Church and were brought by bus. Once again, God took care of our needs!

My oldest son and daughter and I joined them in the yard and we shared fellowship as we worked together. What a wonderful group of young people they were! I told them how they were the hand of God for so many of us in the neighborhood: We had a sick child, the neighbor across the street was battling breast cancer, another neighbor was awaiting surgery, and another neighbor was recently widowed.

Oh most generous and loving God, You know our needs even before we do! Sometimes You send us to help, and sometimes we are to be the recipients of Your generosity.

I found myself remarking to my children once again that we did what we could to help others the day before, and others did what they could to help us the next day. What a marvelous system. God is at work in the Icon Dei Guild, our priests, in the middle school youth group from Kensington Church, in you, and in me.

—**Michele Elena Bondi**

"I Trust In You! Save My Hand"

How quickly Divine Mercy works.

It was late in February 2009 when I arrived home after daily Mass. Hurriedly, I stormed into the kitchen, still wearing all my winter clothes. I had no time to take them off because I had to get my baking done before 1:00 p.m. I had big plans for that afternoon. But my plans were thrashed very soon.

I got all my ingredients ready, placed them one after the other into my big bread-making machine. Up to that point everything went fine. Next, my dough was ready to be checked. I turned the motor off and put my right hand on the very bottom of the bowl. At the same time that I reached for something with my left hand, either my loose cuff on the sleeve of the coat—or whatever or however—something turned the motor switch on with my hand on the bottom, inside the bowl. I was conscious enough to turn the switch off, but it wasn't fast enough.

My right hand was already mangled badly. When I viewed the damage that was done I thought to myself, *Surely I'll lose my hand*, but I did not give up. I knew I needed divine assistance. So I raised my hand up toward Divine Mercy and said, "Merciful Jesus, here's my hand, do with it what's got to be done. I trust in You! Save my hand."

Just at that moment, my phone rang. It was my sister and she was laughing. I told her, "Dee, don't laugh, come quickly. I need you," but she insisted on telling me why she was laughing.

She said, "I'm laughing because I've never called you and had you answer." She said she was calling my other sister. Wow! How quickly Divine Mercy works. Thoughts were going through my mind that if I had to call someone, by the time I would get someone, I probably would have collapsed from loss of blood. But Dee came quickly, I was in the emergency room in no time, and was taken care of right away.

The doctors advised me to be admitted to the hospital. They said I had a very serious injury and was taking a chance with my life. I would not give in and stay in the hospital. Maybe I was plain old stubborn and stupid, but a short time after returning home my whole arm was infected very badly up to my neck. So I went back to the hospital. They hooked me up to several different tubes on my nose, on my arms, and wrist. I was weakened to the point that I passed out. This whole ordeal lasted several hours and I never, for one moment, lost my trust in Divine Mercy.

I felt that things would turn out fine. I kept praying and saying, "Jesus, I trust in You" whenever I was able to. "May Your will be done." Here I am today with my right hand healed. It is not like it used to be, and according to the medical world, it will never be the same again. The main thing is I have my hand, use it, and I had asked Divine Mercy to "save my hand."

May God be praised, blessed and glorified, for the outpouring of His graces upon all who trust in Him.

—LUCY

OUR GOOD FRIDAY MIRACLE

Jesus, thank You for Your great love and mercy!

...He was wounded for our transgressions, crushed for our iniquities; upon him was the punishment that made us whole, and by his bruises we are healed. All we like sheep have gone astray; we have all turned to our own way, and the Lord has laid on Him the iniquity of us all.
—Isaiah 53: 5-6.

On April 2, 2010, my children and I attended the Liturgy of Good Friday at our new parish. Earlier in the year, God told me to bring my children to Mass there. His summons was a big surprise, although I came to understand that it was the answer to my prayers. How perfectly God knows what we need, how He looks after us, how much He loves us!

The night before, my sons were altar boys during the Mass of the Lord's Supper. For the first time in my life I experienced a Mass where I truly felt that I was in Heaven while still upon earth. Someone mentioned that there were 82 altar boys at that Mass. As Mass concluded, the many altar boys lined the main aisle and the priests processed from the altar to the chapel with the Eucharist. What a beautiful, beautiful moment that was on the night we commemorate the institution of the Holy Mass and the priesthood, Holy Thursday.

Just before leaving church that Good Friday, my children and I awaited our turn to venerate the cross. How much easier it would have been to
leave right then instead of awaiting our turn before the cross. Dear Jesus,
how difficult it is to process up and venerate Your cross, to face You and
see what our choices cost You. We did it because we love You! We did it
because of all You did for us.

After returning home following the Liturgy of Good Friday, I hung
up my church clothes and gathered together my clothes for Easter Sunday
Mass. Earlier in the week I had put a pink suit jacket aside because it had
a few small spots on it. On Good Friday while in the laundry room to
clean the jacket I found that the few round brownish dots were gone and
instead, the jacket was covered with many crosses.

 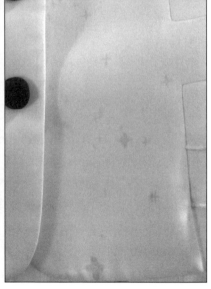

Most loving Savior, by Your Passion, death on a Cross, and Resurrection You have redeemed every single person. How much You love us,
how much You thirst for us to accept Your offer of salvation. Dear Jesus,
I accept and I thank You! May we spend our lives adoring You.

—MICHELE ELENA BONDI

Photos Copyright © 2010 Joseph Karl Publishing.

CHAPTER SEVEN

RECONCILIATION

WHAT IS THE VALUE OF ONE SOUL?

He set the value with His own life because
He loves us that much.

What a month last October was! I threw out my dissertation proposal, my son turned 15, twice I carried the Creator of the Universe in a little pyx to my sister and witnessed the awesome power of God's love at work in her life. I helped my three children find or make costumes for Halloween, readied my son for the Sacrament of Confirmation, and assisted as my small people carved pumpkins.

The adventure continued when I closed yet another chapter in my life. It all had to do with a check made out to me, with my name misspelled.

What is the value of one soul?

About four years ago I hired a lawyer because my family was in great need of someone to assist us in court. The lawyer cashed my retainer fee and that was that, except for the brief time he showed up at the courthouse once to delay the proceedings. He was bleeding from a wound in his head. The next time we were to appear in court the lawyer did not show up. That was very bad news. Without a lawyer to help me defend the truth and my rights, I lost a lot of money. And some rights. But that is another amazing story of the incredible power of God at work in ways we do not always understand.

What is the value of one soul?

At the time I was so sorrowful and angry that my lawyer had stolen from me and my three young Catholic-school students. Money was so tight! I was already frustrated that I had to spend so much money on court nonsense, and then my legal representative took even more! Righteous anger took hold. The children and I have had many discussions since about the ways multiple people are affected by one person's decision to sin. We prayed for the lawyer during Mass and handed over our anger and hurt during the Sacrament of Reconciliation. We discussed the great mercy of God who brought this man to the attention of our family, knowing that we would pray for his eternal soul.

What is the value of one soul?

One year later I filed a grievance with the State Attorney Grievance Commission. Their process for obtaining justice took years. About a year ago I was informed of the lawyer's "changed ways" since being found guilty of stealing. I would have been more convinced had I heard it from him directly, or if he had attempted to pay back what he stole, but *my role was to be the one to forgive, not the one to judge.*

One afternoon my children and I headed for the post office, navigating our way through the streets in the middle of a construction zone while trying to find the building set way back from the road with all the street signs down, guessing where to go—one final inconvenience before finally claiming our money.

The Attorney Grievance Commission awarded us an amount that was half of what the lawyer had stolen. However, God had already returned to us all that we lost and so the money we got back turned into a bonus.

What is the value of one soul?

On the way to the bank, the children and I discussed our continuing need to pray for the man as we seek to live in imitation of Christ. We put the money in an account set aside to pay for the publishing of two new Catholic books for teens and preteens that will emphasize the love of God and remind them that they have an important role to play in salvation history. What a beautiful ending to this story!

Most Compassionate and Merciful God, we remember how You suffered and died for us on the Cross and how You took our sins upon Yourself to satisfy Divine Justice in every one of our places. May we live in imitation of You by praying for all sinners, especially those You bring to our attention. Please forgive us for the times we have sinned against others. **To You, Jesus, the value of one soul is equal to Your Life. You love us that much.**

—MICHELE ELENA BONDI

LOVE THY NEIGHBOR

I hope the poetry I write
Brings a smile to a reader's life.
For a reader is my neighbor,
For whom serves this pen and paper.

And it means a great deal to me
To honor their integrity,
So it is prudence I favor
In pursuit of my endeavor.

I do not for sure remember,
When revered "Mr." and "Mrs.,"
Were displaced by "the consumer,"
An "ID number," "the user."

But I hope one day we'll enter
An era of "love thy neighbor."
Whether a family member,
A customer, a co-worker.

One that will foster courtesy,
Thoughtfulness and sincerity,
That has eager initiative,
And sees things in the positive.

I pray one day all neighborhoods
Become safe places to plant roots,
With homes bought not just for profit,
But "love for the land" as motive.

Places we can always call home,
With friends still living there we know;
And where still sings the ice-cream trucks,
And people sit in their front yards
I hope one day we will enter
An era of "love thy neighbor,"
Where our talents and unique gifts
Are all used for worthy service.

One that will foster honesty,
Patience and generosity,
For we are all precious because,
We're made in the likeness of God.

—BELINDA BONDI
Copyright © 2010 Belinda Bondi

REAL ESTATE ISSUES AND SALVATION

"Jesus, Mary, Joseph, save souls."

A fter receiving a *Pieta* prayer book in 2001 from a kind woman at daily Mass, I learned to say the prayer "Jesus, Mary, Joseph, I love You, save souls." Eager to do my part and grateful for the help I received through the prayers of others, I agreed to be God's instrument in helping others through prayer. Have you ever heard the expression "Be careful what you pray for?"

In 2001 my marriage was ending and our family home was put up for sale. My children and I had to find a new place to live. There are no words suitable to describe the painful moment as we watched the "for sale" sign driven into the ground in the front yard. Placing our family completely in His care, I prayed that God put us where He wanted us. We prayed to St. Joseph for His intercession in the sale of our home and the acquisition of a new one.

For two long years nothing happened. Home sales slowed following the terrorist attacks on 9/11. I would playfully ask St. Joseph if God had his hands tied up there in heaven. The waiting was difficult and painful, but I trusted in God's perfect timing. One day while I was looking at his prayer card, St. Joseph said to me, "I can help you now. Pray." I prayed with delight upon hearing such wonderful news, and someone made an offer on our house. I also continued my regular prayer "Jesus, Mary, Joseph, I love You, save souls." We were finally free to move!

I had become very fond of my real estate agents, who had also lived through the trauma of divorce and seemed interested in my family's welfare during a very difficult time in our lives. They helped me find a house and a mortgage company. Finally, finally, things were improving, we found a home to move to, and were ready to go. As I so often say in my life, I had my plan and God had His plan. We were going to move, but first He had something important to accomplish! God was going to answer my prayer and use my situation to reach out to some of His wayward sheep.

One day a friend asked me how my real estate dealings were going. St. Joseph had sent her to look after us because as it turned out, my mortgage company had promised me one type of mortgage and then changed the rate and type of loan while adding on expensive fees. In their pride, they thought that I would not know the difference. I did not know the difference, but God did! He sent my friend before the deal was done to prevent us from being cheated out of our much-needed money. As soon as I found out, I called a meeting with the mortgage people, including the head of the company, his Catholic son (who tried to intimidate me by reminding me that he was also a lawyer), and the Catholic young man I had been working with who seemed increasingly uncomfortable each time I met with him.

There the men sat in their expensive suits, using tactics of intimidation to steal money from a young family they knew were vulnerable. They arrogantly asked me how I found out about the switch and the fees, and you should have seen their faces when I told them that St. Joseph was our intercessor! God spoke through me as I called the men on their brazen thievery and dishonesty. I told the men the story of Jesus overturning the tables in the temple, and the young lawyer exonerated himself by stating that he had gone to Catholic school and knew of the story. He insisted on using the faulty and immoral logic that cheating people in the name of business is somehow defensible.

Jesus, Mary, Joseph, I love You, save souls.

Joseph was not only overseeing that our relocation went well, he was interceding for the souls of these men and our real estate agents who allowed it to happen. St. Joseph was making sure we were not cheated by thieves stealing in the name of good business. The men were shocked as God called them on their crooked behavior, using as His instrument a young mother with a preschooler on her lap! The deal on the house we were going to buy fell through because of the deceit of the mortgage people.

Later, while speaking of the turn of events to my shocked Realtor, I pointed out that to her that all the people involved were putting their very souls at risk by cheating people out of money and God was not pleased. Her jaw nearly hit the floor! Rather than earn an honest income by living in imitation of Christ, they all ended up fired. Once that was accomplished, St. Joseph found us a cheaper house and we acquired a mortgage from an honest and reputable company.

By the time the dishonest deal to buy our next home fell through, we were served with an eviction notice by the new owner of our former home who wanted to take possession. The way it played out, we had one day to find another house. What a time of suffering that was for us! Our new Realtor prayed to Our Lady, and the day we moved in she told me about her prayers and noted that the name of our new street has Mary's name in it.

I had one request for God pertaining to our new home: that we end up on a lot with a nice backyard where my children could play. Doesn't God love to delight us? Through His servant St. Joseph, He put us in a pretty neighborhood with mature trees and kind neighbors, on a lot with a roomy, tree-lined backyard. There was even a delightful playscape for my children to play on with not just one slide, but two! We moved in early spring, and were enchanted as the delightful flowers presented themselves one by one in the lovely flowerbeds. In every flower I saw the face of Jesus smiling at us. One year later, one of my dearest friends moved in right across the street. The power of St. Joseph is mighty because he is backed up by the power of our most loving and honest God. This year we will celebrate the six-year anniversary of living in our delightful home.

Thank you, God, thank you, St. Joseph! We love it here. Jesus, Mary, Joseph, I love You, keep saving souls.

—MICHELE ELENA BONDI

JESUS, THE JUST JUDGE

His love and mercy are the ultimate authority.

Six years ago I joined a divorce support group at a local Catholic church where I was tremendously blessed to meet a young mother who quickly became a close friend. She and I were going through very similar circumstances and our paths continued to run parallel. Together we saw each other through the long, drawn-out legal termination of dysfunctional marriages and the years of subsequent persecution inside and outside of the courthouse.

Our friendship was of priceless value to me. My friend and I shared many happy memories together with our children as we reclaimed our freedom and tried to live as normal lives as possible under the circumstances. We supported each other, vacationed together, had many celebrations at each other's homes, attended school functions and worshipped together, and prayed for each other. We watched each other's children and collaborated as our lives evolved. We supported each other through many unnecessary court battles and were able to offer each other compassion and understanding.

One morning my friend and I saw our children off to school and then traveled to the courthouse where she was once again forced to defend herself against more persecution. Like so many families who find themselves in family court, my friend and I thought at first that we would get justice and the protection that our families desperately needed there. Instead, many innocent families are further harmed by the family court system that abusers manipulate to batter their families, sometimes until the children reach the age of 18. That is what happened to our families. Unfortunately, the judges and referees involved in our cases were not interested in hearing the truth. More often than not, their decisions helped our abusers batter us.

When a person who is being battered by someone is forced to fight in court, the experience is physically and emotionally exhausting, very, very expensive, and very damaging to the children. Your parental rights can be taken from you at any time and decisions that should be yours to make are made by complete strangers who may or may not have your child's best interest in mind. Often power and money decide what is "best" for the children. Usually there is little respect for the dignity of people and cases are decided abruptly, often with little investigation, and little or no concern for the truth. The rules of engagement are never made clear. For decent families whose abusers use the court system as a weapon, family court is the worst place to be and your God-given right to parent your children are returned to you when their childhood is over.

My friend and I entered the courtroom and took a seat in the back to await her turn. Often we did not know where to go or when we could expect to be seen. Concerns about childcare while you were at court were of no concern to anyone. You had to show up if the children happened to be sick and you had better not bring them with you. Sometimes you go before a judge, sometimes you see someone else. You may have been scheduled to see a judge but could end up before a referee or a mediator or your case may not be heard that day at all.

If you fail to hire an attorney to preserve your family's much-needed resources and instead defend yourself, you could be at a severe disadvantage. If you have a lawyer, it costs you plenty and you give up the right to speak for yourself, but in our cases no one wanted to hear what we had to say anyway. There were so many others waiting and we got the sense that the judges and referees were sick of listening to everyone, no matter what their circumstances.

Eventually my friend was called to go before the judge. She walked up to the table before the judge's bench and sat down while her ex-husband and his lawyer also approached the judge's bench and took seats by the plaintiff's table on the right. My friend was in the bad position of having to defend herself and her children against people who were willing to pay a lot of money and lie to win at all costs. That strategy gets results in the courthouse. Good luck to you if you are persecuted and your defense is the truth.

The judge sat behind her large desk, which was elevated above the people she was there to serve. Man's laws elevated to a high degree so often are not laboring for God's truths to help people. Greed and the quest for control and revenge were the law of the land in our experiences. My friend looked so small before the judge sitting above her. As we often did for each other, I prayed to God to protect my friend and her children. God had always provided for our families. However, the persecution against my kind friend and her beautiful children continued, year after year, with no end in sight. This ongoing battering using the court as a weapon was tremendously draining for her mentally, physically, and financially and was extremely damaging to her children. She longed to be free from the torment so she and the children could be free to live normal lives. What would happen this time?

Oftentimes we had left court not sure exactly what had happened and what the fallout would be. The complexity of the legal system harms good people. One thing we both could be certain of after every appearance in court was that more persecution would follow. Realizing that anything could happen, we always approached our court battering unsure of what the ruling would be. One thing that was certain was that we could not expect compassion. Fortunately we had each other to talk things out with before and after our court appearances. We also had God!

The judge asked some questions as my friend and I powerlessly followed along with the proceedings. The other party vehemently presented and defended his case, desperate to win the right to control other people. Things were not going well for my friend. Then, an image appeared behind the judge.

I stared, looked away, and then looked again to see if the image was still there. *Yes it was!* Behind the judge, who had looked so large and prominent elevated above the people she was there to serve, was the image of Jesus in profile. His image was huge and dwarfed the judge! After all was said and done my friend and I stepped outside to figure out what the ruling was and what it meant for her and her children. I joyfully informed her that Jesus had made His Presence known in the courtroom on her behalf. He was with her!

God in His mercy revealed Himself to assure her that Jesus loves families and was looking out for them. He made it clear that day that He is truth and justice and the One whom we should go to when we make our decisions. What great mercy to reveal Himself to His beloved and offer comfort and hope while providing us with His strength. When we do what is right we can be assured that God remains with us and will provide everything He sees fit in His most perfect plan. My friend continues to be forced to fight for justice as she hopes for peace and prays for the souls of those who have lost their way.

—ANONYMOUS

How I Rejected Jesus on My Way to Mass

That was a terrible, terrible moment.

When one turns one's life over to God completely, life can end up being many things other than what one had planned. That is what I had faced through the previous three weeks and often before that. Yesterday before making my way to the 5 o'clock Mass, I decided to have dinner at one of my favorite places and play with some ideas for a charming film in development.

While waiting for the food I readied my equipment and put a CD into the computer. My food arrived, I settled in, put earphones in to listen to music options, and started eating. The food tasted all the more delicious because I had not eaten much that day. I contemplated for a moment how blessed I was to be enjoying such a delightful meal and thanked God for His generosity. I was mindful of the one-hour fast before receiving Holy Communion, and there was not much time to eat and consider my project before having to leave for the church.

At that point a man came into the rather empty establishment and sat down right by me. I was aware of his presence and had already made up my mind to stick to my project because time was short. I really wanted to be left alone. The man started talking to me but I wanted no part in the conversation.

169

Wishing that this was not happening, I turned toward the man knowing that the earphones in my ears would be my way out of the situation. I said to the man very curtly, "I can't hear you," pointed to my earphones, and turned back to my computer and my food. Often, people approach me while I work (the world is my office), and despite all the work on the table, will talk to me at great length anyway. Sometimes I do that to other people. Yesterday was the first time that I was unwilling to be flexible.

The man sat in the chair for a little while longer. I immediately felt deeply remorseful for my behavior. Granted, the man looked rough and I was concerned at least a little for my safety. My food no longer tasted good and the project no longer seemed fun. Soon the man got up and left the building, carried his backpack to his bicycle and slowly walked away without getting on it. As he walked away, I saw Jesus walking away from me. *By rejecting my brother, I had rejected Jesus!*

There are no words to describe to you what I felt like. I admonished myself severely for sending Jesus away just as I was headed for Mass. What if He sent that man inside, to me, so the man could receive a meal? How long had it been since he had eaten? How many others had rejected him before me? Perhaps he was a veteran! Great was my sorrow as I packed up my things, including the delicious food I could no longer enjoy in good conscience. Perhaps I had sent my brother away hungry when I had been given so much, while on my way to Holy Mass!

Throughout the Mass I felt so ashamed of my behavior. As a Catholic I am called to live in imitation of Christ. As a member of the Catholic Church I am obligated to be His instrument and a living witness of my faith. Jesus, You have blessed me with so many gifts that have been given so freely. *May I never, ever again send You away rejected or hungry!*

—MICHELE ELENA BONDI

Thank God for Second Chances

This time, I was all smiles.

When a person hands one's life over to God, that life becomes many different things: interesting, different, astounding, humbled, forever altered in ways one would perhaps never have expected. One finds oneself traveling in directions that were never on the personal road map or navigation device. Things are seen that were never before on one's personal radar. In some respects one may get used to it. In some ways one will be immensely challenged. With obedience comes grace, peace, a sense of purpose, joy, inspiration, and consolation.

My children and I enjoyed a delightful lunch together at a local restaurant. We discussed our plans for the future as we hear God calling us to make some major changes. As we were leaving I bent down to pick something up off the floor by our table. My oldest son Andre remarked that at first he thought I was genuflecting. We all smiled and acknowledged the possibility of that actually happening as we live our lives with gratitude to God and recognize His constant presence among us.

We do not always have to get it right. However, we must be obedient for God's plans to come to fruition through us. During lunch with a

171

friend earlier in the week the conversation included my remorse at having rejected Jesus on my way to Mass the weekend before. My friend sagely reassured me and said not to worry, for I would run into the rejected man again. I laughed, because despite the fact that I had never seen the man before, I know that with God all things are possible!

So it came to pass that the next day I had one hour to grab a cup of coffee and a scone at a local coffee shop and work on a video in production. Everything came to pass so perfectly. I got a front-row parking spot right by the door, acquired a large, vacant table by an outlet, the very table I had been hoping for. I sat down with my coffee and food, the work on the table before me, exactly the scene from that last Sunday! I was once again ready to enjoy my food and drink while working on a video, once again very grateful, once again sitting in the same spot, once again eager to finish a project, once again having very little time for it all.

Then it happened all over again. A man came over to the other side of my table and started talking to me. Within the one second it took me to look up from my computer I knew it would be the same man I treated so terribly on my way to Mass, and it was. I am not sure the man recognized me from our previous encounter, but I recognized him. What joy I felt at seeing the man once again, and for a second chance to be kind.

Granted, the man was a little on the crude side and he did just about all of the talking, but I was all smiles. He asked if he could join me at the table. I pushed my work aside, asked for his name, listened, and kept smiling. This generated many looks from the people around us. I was so happy to be a true witness of the love of God this time. I was given a second chance to love Jesus in return by being kind to my brother.

Eventually I had to leave, and bid the man farewell by name. My children asked me later if I bought the man a meal this time. I am so proud of them for having asked that question. I shook my head and told them that the thought never even occurred to me. At that moment what seemed most paramount was the importance of feeding his soul.

My children and I went to Reconciliation where I formally apologized to God for rejecting Jesus on my way to Mass. Now I am forgiven and accept the challenge to live the Greatest Commandment as a witness of God's love always present in the world.

He said to him, "You shall love the Lord your God with all your heart, and with all your soul, and with all your mind." This is the greatest and first commandment. And a second is like it: "You shall love your neighbor as yourself." On these two commandments hang all the law and the prophets." Matthew 22: 37-40

We are called to love every single person, in Jesus' name.

—MICHELE ELENA BONDI

My Prayer Before Reconciliation

Oh sweet Author of Life,
Your pardon I seek as I kneel before Your Cross.
Lord, forgive me.
Immerse me in Your compassion,
for I have so little to offer you.
Even my petition for forgiveness comes from You.

You long for my approach, though wounded,
so generously willing to exchange human iniquity
with the Love that annihilates and saves,
when the soul but accepts Your invitation.
I give my nothingness entirely to You.

Divine Justice, have mercy on me,
and may all my brothers and sisters benefit also,
especially those most in need of Your saving grace.
Blood of Christ wash over me,
and transform my self into You.
Make of me the mirror
that reflects Your love to Your beloved.

I thank You for Your sacrifice and invitation,
for Your patience while awaiting my response,
as I seek Your will
while You encourage me to make my own choices.
For lovingly creating, guiding, and consoling me,
for all You have generously given me,
including the grace to recognize
that which on my own I cannot see.

For allowing me to lose, that I may win.
For giving me the opportunity to journey with You
along Your Way of the Cross.
I accept Your love,
and return to You my heart united with Yours
along with my obedience.

Thank You for everything, Thy will be done;
accept my petition to fill this dry well
with Your Divine Presence.

Amen.

—MICHELE ELENA BONDI
Copyright © 2009 Joseph Karl Publishing

COACH IN IMITATION OF CHRIST

As Catholics, it is our obligation.

My boys Andre and Nick both played basketball last season for their Catholic middle school. How happy they were to be playing basketball along with their peers for their school and for God! One child had a wonderful experience and one had a terrible experience. One had a coach who behaved in imitation of Christ and one did not.

Andre's coach gave each boy a basketball with his name on it at the first practice. He began each practice with the team on its knees praying the "Our Father" and praying for the children's special intentions. While the display was Christian in theory, his behavior on the court was not Christ-like at all.

Andre went to every practice and to every game unless he was sick. He shook the coach's hand and thanked him after every practice. I was very proud of my son. During that terrible season, he acted in imitation of Christ and set a fine example of what it is to be truly Catholic. During practices Andre was chosen to sit out more than the other boys. One boy on the team also played hockey at the same time, often came to practice significantly late, yet the coach played him often. Once that same boy was late for a game because he also had a hockey game that same day, and as soon as he arrived he was put in the game and played frequently.

Often Andre played for one minute the entire game. A few times he played for a total of three minutes. As if that was not bad enough, the coach was mean. I believe that his intentions were good, but he was mean to the boys and mean to the parents of the children whom he did not play. I spoke to the coach about playing Andre more often, but the problem was he and I did not share a belief in one basic principle: Coaching should be done in imitation of Christ. He wanted to coach his way, not Christ's way. He believed in the "win-at-all-costs" philosophy.

The parents of the boys who played most of the time shared that same philosophy. The problem is they were teaching their children incorrectly and that is a serious mistake. Even when the team was losing by a lot, the coach still would not let the other boys play. Imagine the scene as the boys pleaded with the coach from the bench for the opportunity to play while he ignored them.

Nick's coach did not start practice out with a prayer, nor did he buy the boys a basketball. He gave the boys something even better: He coached in imitation of Christ. He treated the boys with respect and dignity. He gave every boy an opportunity to play and the team was still competitive. He was fair and did not show favoritism. He had the same mix of boys on the team with differing skill levels. Both teams had a similar record at the end of the season. The coach Nick had was a fine example of what sports leadership should be. He demonstrated that coaching in imitation of Christ and having a good season is possible. He was greatly liked and respected. Nick learned many wonderful things from his coach, which brought us all great joy.

When children play a CYO sport, the obligation to the families is enormous: $100 fee to play, a one-time $75 fee for the uniform, gas expense (which can add up as CYO games take place at considerable distances from home), participation in 50/50 raffles to raise funds for the host school, concessions (another fundraiser), and the cost of admission to every game. If family and friends attend, they also pay to get there and to get in, and often generously participate in the fundraisers. The time commitment is huge. There are many practices and weekend games. A weekend away game dominates the entire day because of travel time to the game and back, arriving 45 minutes early, plus game time. Younger siblings, friends, and family sacrifice in addition to the parents to support the child, his or her team, and the school.

We decided to give Catholic basketball one more try this year. On the night of tryouts, all the parents and children were told "every child gets to play." We were reassured by what we had heard. Although I would not have thought it possible, the coaching was even worse than Andre's coach. Nick's coach was very punitive, and one mother told me her child complained of stomachaches before practice because he was so upset by what the coach told the boys about being late. If one child was late for practice, all the boys were punished for it. When I took that up with the coach, he said that is the way all his coaches did it when he was younger.

I discussed how punitive measures are neither motivating nor empowering, but he would not listen. Expletives were used against the children on game day, in the locker room where the parents could not hear. The first game of the season we traveled far to the game, got there early, had family attend, paid for admission, waited patiently for the game, bought raffle tickets (and it was not even our school we were supporting), and cheered for the whole team. Nick was not allowed to play at all.

The family we sat next to had a disabled sibling of the player there waiting patiently the whole time to watch the game, and their child never played either. Not even once. The great aunt of another boy who came and paid to get in watched her nephew play for one minute.

After the game, my mother told the coach his behavior was "shameful" and she was right. I told the coach that not playing some of the boys at all was wrong. He would not entertain for one second the possibility that perhaps he was wrong. Unfortunately, he responded by criticizing my son just as he criticized the boys during practices.

Like Andre's coach the year before, he was furious that I would dare speak up against the injustice. My son left the game in tears. I noticed which boys never even got to play, and was disgusted when a family whose child played most of the game said to us, "Great game!" I challenged them to speak up for the boys who never got a chance to play at all. They never did, because they do not live in imitation of Christ either. What is the goal of sports? Why do we put our children on teams, anyway? To be mistreated, to be taught to win at all costs, to learn false pride? Not my family.

There is a "24-Hour Rule" at the school that states parents must wait 24 hours before contacting the coach with an issue. I agree with this rule if the parents are not happy with the score, or felt that the coach should have tucked in his shirt, or they wanted to buy him a hot dog during the game and were disappointed they did not get the opportunity. However, coaches who do not coach in imitation of Christ hide behind this rule and misuse it because they do not want to change their incorrect way of behaving. A Christ-like coach will listen, admit when a mistake has been made, and change his behavior. No child or parent who is victimized by a coach should ever have to wait 24 hours to speak up for justice. No Christ-like coach would ever want them to!

How sad that Nick's coach, whose parents spent tens of thousands of dollars on a Catholic-school education, used such punitive measures to train the children how to coach incorrectly. He used expletives on the children, expected them to give of themselves completely and yet returned to them so little. Perhaps parents and Catholic educators need to take inventory and make serious changes in programs that are not teaching in imitation of Christ. I made the easy decision to take my son out of CYO basketball. I had put him in to learn to live in imitation of Christ, but to learn it incorrectly is more damaging than to not learn it at all.

How many children go on to play professional sports? A miniscule minority. However, every single child has an apostolate, and we need to insist that the philosophy of coaching is one that promotes justice, fairness, motivation via positive reinforcement, and healthy competition.

While talking to Nick's coach on the phone after respecting the "24-Hour Rule," I was told my son would be required to attend every practice, pay to get there and to get into games, and work hard but there was no guarantee that he would play *at all* in any given game. Apparently the athletic department neglected to inform the coaches of what they said to the parents and the boys before tryouts: "Every child plays."

Nick and I discussed the matter with people we respect and asked the coach to relieve us of the commitment we made when we started the season, and so he did. At school the boys on Nick's team called him a "quitter." I explained to him that it is not surprising, as that is what the boys are learning from the coaches who refuse to coach in imitation of Christ, and that is why he did the right thing by leaving that environment. I insist that he learn to behave in a way that is truly Catholic, for one day I will stand before God and will be held accountable. And there will be no "24-Hour Rule" for me or for anyone else to hide behind.

Sure, winning is motivating and fun. Balance in sports is what we must seek. The winning-at-all-costs mentality teaches children to get what they want, when they want it, how they want it, instead of teaching them to work as a team, to be fair, and to be gracious losers. Sometimes the best lessons can be found in a heartbreaking loss, and we close ourselves off to those important teaching moments—in fact we lose them entirely—when we teach the children that winning is the most important part of the game. It is time to take the false pride out of sports and reclaim the game for our children!

Adults are vital role models and it is our behavior that teaches children how to behave, far more than what we say. Our behavior must truly reflect what we pray for. Children and their parents who see through the errors have the right to speak up against them. We are *obligated* to speak up against them. That right should never be taken from us, and the sports leadership needs to pay attention to who is leaving and ask itself, "Why?"

Coach in imitation of Christ.

—MICHELE ELENA BONDI

CONCLUSION:
HIS MASTERPIECES ARE CONSTANTLY ON DISPLAY

There is a show going on at this very moment!

Give 30 people a project and marvel at the 30 different ideas you get back. Teachers know this very well. How fun it must be to give an assignment and delight in the many diverse interpretations that are handed in.

Once a year my children's school hosted an art show, science expo, and cultural fair all on the same night. That event was my very favorite. What happy memories my children and I have of walking from the gym to the cafeteria and back again, browsing the many displays showcasing so much talent! Last year the theme for the art show was "Reach for the Star." That one theme was represented in ceramics, drawings, paintings, piano compositions, mosaics, photography, woodwork, and many other ideas.

The participants in the cultural fair celebrate cultures from around the globe. Last year there were displays, performances, clothing, and food from many different countries. My children's displays focused on the Catholic faith in three different countries and listed the saints from each one. The science fair has many diverse experiments and collections. Relativity, gravity, propulsion, geology—how fun to see them investigated and interpreted by the young. In each of the three categories of art, science, and culture, not one entry has ever been exactly the same.

The event led me to think about how we delight in creating, problem solving, designing, and experimenting. We appreciate the creation of something wonderful and a job well done. Now imagine God at the moment when He decided to create something that He loves very much: us! God, Master of Creation and Teacher, gave Himself the task of creating people. One by one He thought us up, and none of us came out the same!

Think about the time God spent on you. Perhaps He started out dreaming of your many talents and the role your apostolate would play in His plan of salvation. Imagine the anticipation God felt and how excited He was through all time for your moment to be born! How much He loved you as He waited. God must have rejoiced in the waiting, knowing that was the perfect timing for your life.

Imagine how happy He was to share the world He created for you to live in. Sunrises and sunsets, flowers, animals, plants, streams, breezes. Do you think every time a new person is created there is a celebration in heaven? I bet that God celebrates on your birthday. He rejoices with the angels, saints, and all in Heaven, and there is singing and music playing, because what God creates is good. Share in the delight God has for every person He created. His works are constantly on display and there is a show going on every moment. Admission is always free.

Consider this, from Fulton J. Sheen:

> Only let us not be fooled by those who say human life has no purpose, and who, in the language of a scientist, say that life is like a lit candle and that when the candle is done the flame goes out, and that is the end of us all. But what this scientist forgot to tell us is that light is not something in the candle, but something that emanates from it; something associated with matter

but separable and distinct from it. For even when the candle has burned out, the light continues to emit itself at the rate of 186,000 miles a second, beyond the moon and stars, beyond the Pleiades, the nebulas of Andromeda, and continues to do so as long as the universe endures.

And so when the candle of our life burns low, may we have kept our soul so free, that like a flame it will leap upwards to the Great Fire at which it was enkindled, and never stop until its light meets that Heavenly Light that ages ago came to this world as its Light, to teach us all to say at the end of our earthly pilgrimage here, as He said at the close of His: 'Father, into Thy Hands I commend My Spirit.'[13]

This compilation of God moments was commissioned for you by our ever-present, infinitely loving God. When you or someone you know or do not know is in need of encouragement, offer them the love of God, which is all-encompassing, never-ending, and can never be contained. God is at work in you!

—MICHELE ELENA BONDI
Before the Blessed Sacrament

---

13 Fulton J. Sheen, *The Rainbow of Sorrow* (Garden City, NY: Garden City Books, 1953), p. 93-94.

REFERENCES

The Scripture quotations contained herein are from the *New Revised Standard Version Bible*, copyright 1989, by the Division of Christian Education of the National Council of the Churches of Christ in the U.S.A. Used by permission. All rights reserved.

1. Fulton J. Sheen, *The Divine Romance* (New York: Alba House, 1996).

2. St. Therese of Lisieux, *The Story of a Soul* (Rockford, IL: Tan Books and Publishers, 1997).

3. Rev. John F. Russell, O. Carm., The Path to Spiritual Maturity: St. Therese of Lisieux (Niagara Falls: Society of the Little Flower, www.littleflower.org).

4. Linda J. Perakis, *Led By the Holy Spirit* (Deckerville, MI: Pine Cone Press, 2004). Reprinted with permission.

5. Compiled and Arranged by W.M.B., *Thoughts of The Cure'D'Ars* (Rockford, IL: Tan Books and Publishers, Inc., 1967).

6. Compiled and Arranged by W.M.B., *Thoughts of The Cure'D'Ars* (Rockford, IL: Tan Books and Publishers, Inc., 1967).

7. Karen Kingsbury, *A Treasury of Miracles for Teens: True Stories of God's Presence Today* (Warner Faith, 2003).

8. Maria von Trapp, *Maria: My Own Story* (Carol Stream, IL: Creation House, 1972).

9. Fulton J. Sheen, *The Way of the Cross* (Huntington, IN: Our Sunday Visitor, 1982).

10. Compiled and Arranged by W.M.B., *Thoughts of The Cure 'D 'Ars* (Rockford, IL: Tan Books and Publishers, Inc., 1967).

11. Compiled and Arranged by W.M.B., *Thoughts of The Cure 'D 'Ars* (Rockford, IL: Tan Books and Publishers, Inc., 1967).

12. Compiled and Arranged by W.M.B., *Thoughts of The Cure 'D 'Ars* (Rockford, IL: Tan Books and Publishers, Inc., 1967)

13. Fulton J. Sheen, *The Rainbow of Sorrow* (Garden City, NY: Garden City Books, 1953).

ACKNOWLEDGEMENTS

My dear Lord, I thank You for manifesting Your infinite love through so many "God moments" and pray this work is pleasing in Your sight. All honor and glory to You, Most High Triune God!

What a tremendous blessing it has been to journey through life, sharing so much love and so many God moments, with those nearest and dearest to me including my mother Herta Bondi, sister Belinda Bondi, aunt Laura Bondi, children Andre, Nick, and Alyssa Bottesi, and brother Joe, sister-in-law Pam, and nieces Allison and Morgan Bondi.

I extend my gratitude to the exceptional team of people who brought this book to fruition including editors Susan S., Gene X. Kortsha, graphic designer Roseann Nieman, book layout, design, and editor Erin Howarth, book consultant and proof-reader Nancy Carabio Belanger, and George Piliouras, communications. Working with each of you has been such a pleasure and has brought me great joy.

Lastly, I am grateful to the wonderful people who shared their God moments in this book: Nancy Carabio Belanger, Belinda Bondi, Rejeanne Buckley, Chris Camilli, Sharon Rose Cecil, Lynn Czar, Teresa Koempel, Gene Kortsha, Ted, Lucy, George Madrid Sr., and Linda J. Perakis.

God is at work in you!

Most sincerely,

Michele Elena Bondi

AWARD-WINNING BOOKS BY MICHELE ELENA BONDI:

Your Personal Apostolate: Accepting and Sharing the Love of God
2010 Catholic Press Association Book Award-winner

Your Teen Apostolate: Accepting and Sharing the Love of God
(with Andre J. Bottesi)
2010 Catholic Press Association Book Awards
Best Children's Book
Best Family Life Book

Your Preteen Apostolate: Accepting and Sharing the Love of God
(with Nicholas J. Bottesi)
2010 Catholic Press Association Book Awards
Best Children's Book
Best Family Life Book

Books available from Joseph Karl Publishing
www.Godisatworkinyou.com